A-Z CA

C000245395

CO

Key to Map Pages	Back C
Large Scale Pages	
Map Pages	4-33

Index to Colleges and Halls 48

REFERENCE

Motorway	M11
A Road	A14
B Road	B1049
Dual Carriageway	
One-way Street Traffic flow on A Roads is indicated by a heavy line on the drivers left	
Restricted Access	
Pedestrianized Road	
Residential Walkway	
Track & Footpath	
Railway	Level Crossing X Station ⊟
Local Authority Boundary	— · — · —
Postcode Boundary	— · · — · · —
Built-up Area	MILL ST.
Map Continuation	20 Large Scale City Centre 2
Car Park (selected)	P
Church or Chapel	†
Cycle Route	🚴
Fire Station	■

Hospital	H
House Numbers A & B Roads Only	83 96
Information Centre	🛈
National Grid Reference	⁵45
Park & Ride	Cowley Road P+🚌
Police Station	▲
Post Office	★
Safety Camera with Speed Limit Fixed cameras and long term road works cameras Symbols do not indicate camera direction	30
Toilet without facilities for the Disabled with facilities for the Disabled	▽ ▽
Educational Establishment	
Hospital or Healthcare Building	
Industrial Building	
Leisure or Recreational Facility	
Cambridge University, College/Hall	
Place of Interest	
Public Building	
Shopping Centre or Market	
Other Selected Buildings	

SCALE

Map Pages 4-33	1:16,896
0	¼ Mile
0 250 500 Metres	
3¾ inches (9.52cm) to 1 mile	5.92 cm to 1 kilometre

Map Pages 2-3	1:8,448
0	⅛ Mile
0 125 250 Metres	
7½ inches (19.05cm) to 1 mile	11.84 cm to 1 kilometre

Copyright of Geographers' A-Z Map Company Limited

Fairfield Road, Borough Green, Sevenoaks, Kent TN15 8PP
Telephone: 01732 781000 (Enquiries & Trade Sales)
01732 783422 (Retail Sales)
www.a-zmaps.co.uk
Copyright © Geographers' A-Z Map Co. Ltd.
Edition 4 2009

Ordnance Survey® This product includes mapping data licensed from Ordnance Survey® with the permission of the Controller of Her Majesty's Stationery Office.

© Crown Copyright 2008. All rights reserved. Licence number 100017302
Safety camera information supplied by www.PocketGPSWorld.com
Speed Camera Location Database Copyright 2008 © PocketGPSWorld.com

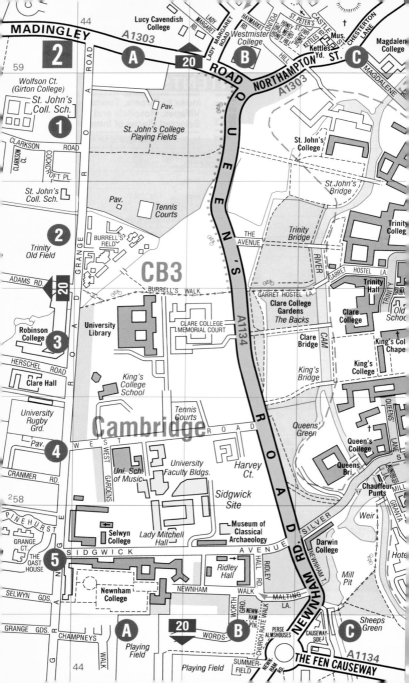

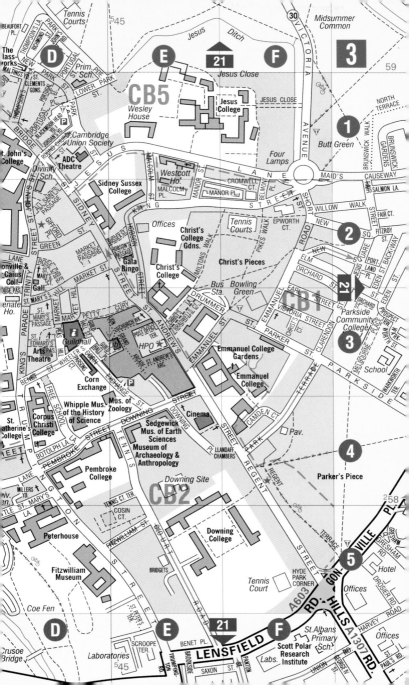

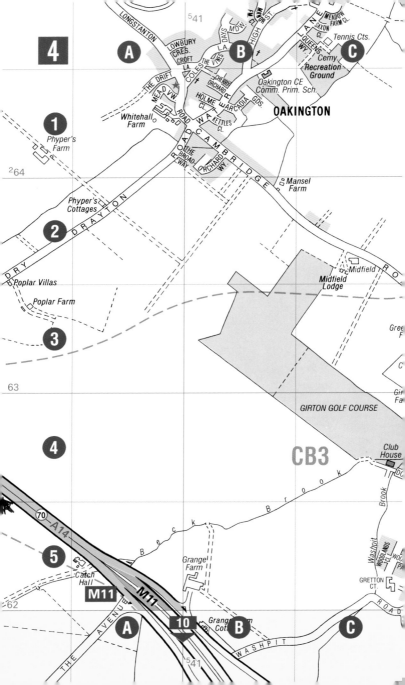

4

A

B

C

LONGSTANTON

⁵41

LOWBURY
CRES.
CROFT
LA.

THE DRIFT

MEAD VW.

Whitehall
Farm

THE VINES

DAYS

COLES LA.

CHERRY
ORCHARD

HOLME
CL.

ARCADIA
GDS.

KETTLES
CL.

HIGH ST.

MDW.

WINDMILL ST.

MEADOW
FARM CL.

SAXON
CL.

QUEENS
WY.

LANE

Cemy.

Tennis Cts.

Recreation
Ground

C

Oakington CE
Comm. Prim. Sch.

OAKINGTON

1

Phyper's
Farm

²64

THE
BROAD
WY.

ORCHARD
WY.

BROADWAY

CAMBRIDGE ROAD

² Mansel
Farm

Phyper's
Cottages

DRAYTON

2

DRY

Poplar Villas

Poplar Farm

3

Midfield

Midfield
Lodge

ROAD

Gree

63

Gir
Fa

C'

GIRTON GOLF COURSE

4

CB3

Club
House

D

70 A14

Brook

Brook

Washpit

WOODLANDS CL.

WOO

5

Catch
Hall

M11

M11

Beck

Grange
Farm

GRETTON
CT.

ROAD

⁶2

THE AVENUE

A

10

Grange m
Cott

B

WASHPIT

C

⁵41

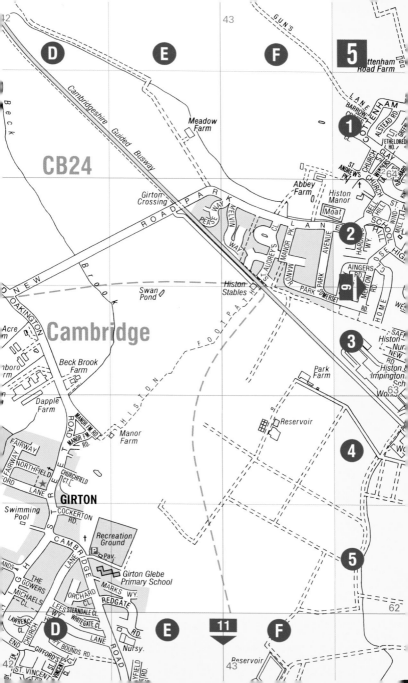

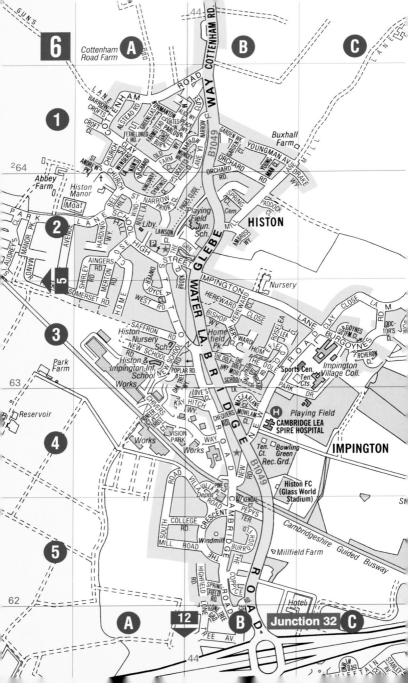

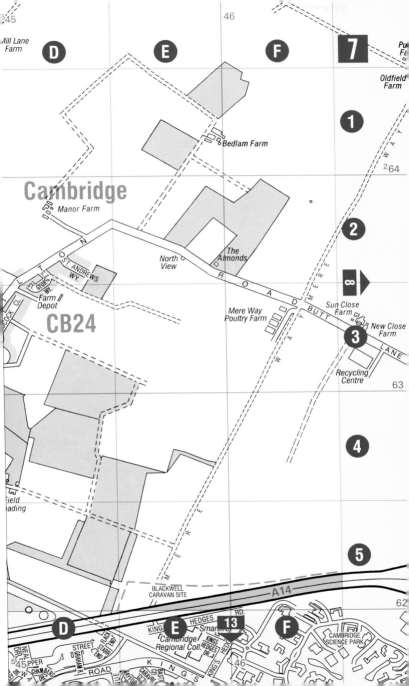

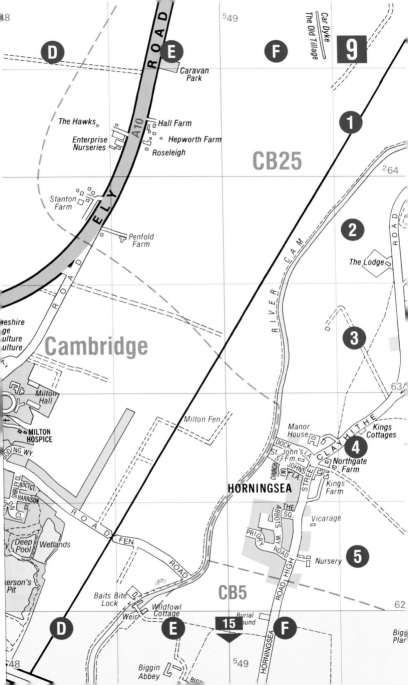

D   548   **E**   549   **F**

Car Dyke
The Old Tillage

9

1

Caravan
Park

The Hawks
Hall Farm

Enterprise
Nurseries
Hepworth Farm

Roseleigh

CB25

264

2

The Lodge

Stanton
Farm

Penfold
Farm

RIVER CAM

3

ROAD

ELY ROAD   A10

Cambridge

63

CLAYHITHE

Milton Fen

eshire
ge
ulture
ulture

Milton
Hall

Manor
House

Kings
Cottages

DOCK LA.
St. John's
Fm.
4

Northgate
Farm

CHURCH
END

JOHNS

LA.

STREET

Kings
Farm

**MILTON
HOSPICE**

DING WY.

HORNINGSEA

THE
SQ.

Vicarage

BOCT CT.

HARRISON
CL.

SHIRLEY CL.
CL.

PRIORY

ABBOTS WY.
ROAD

ROAD

Nursery

5

Deep
Pool

Wetlands

FEN

ROAD

HIGH

HORNINGSEA ROAD

erson's
Pit

CB5

62

Baits Bite
Lock

Weir

Wildfowl
Cottage

Burial
Ground

15

Biggin
Abbey

Bigg
Plar

D   548   **E**   549   **F**

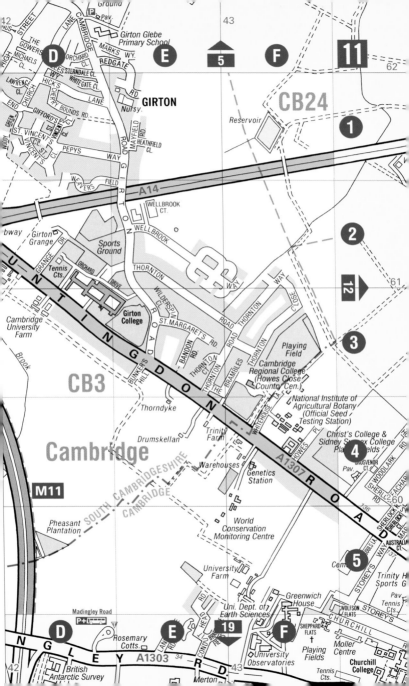

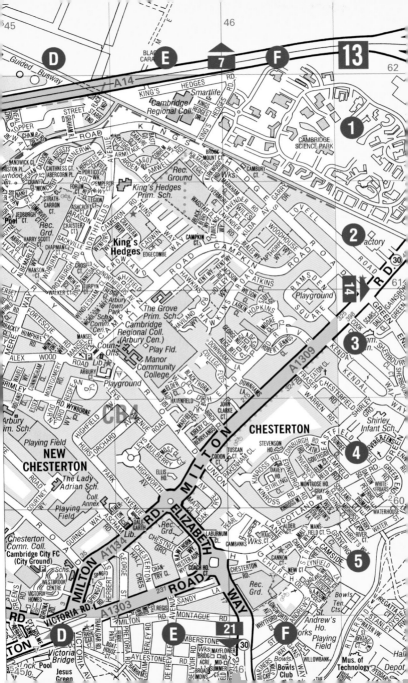

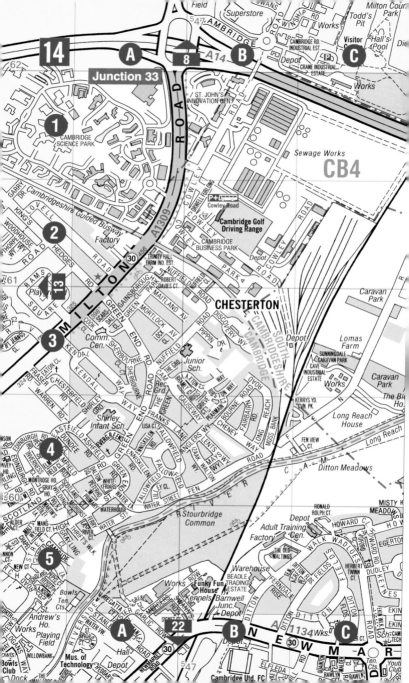

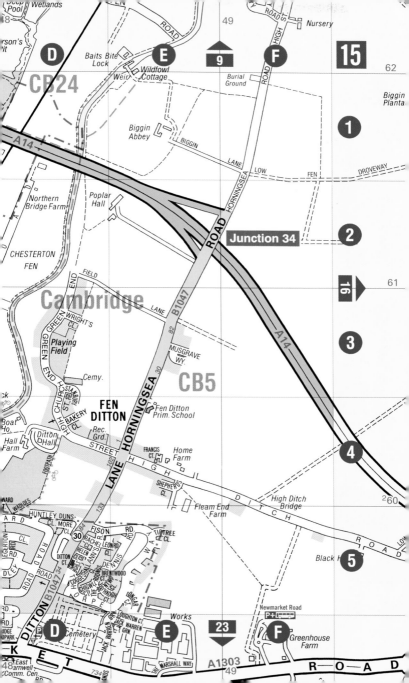

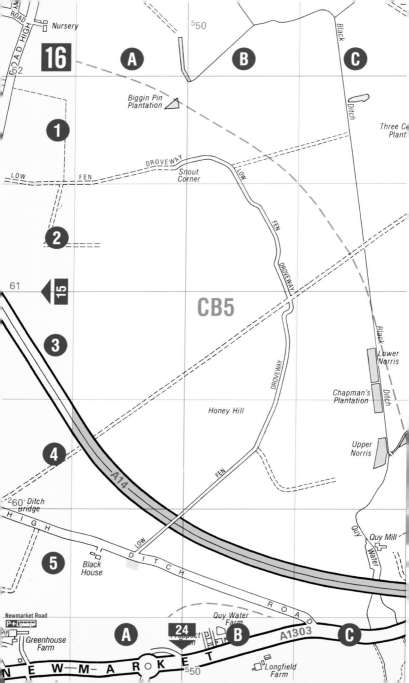

ROAD HIGH

Nursery

550

16

A

B

C

62

Black

Biggin Pin
Plantation

Ditch

Three C
Plant

1

DROVEWAY

LOW

FEN

Snout
Corner

LOW

2

FEN

DROVEWAY

61

◄ 15

CB5

3

DROVEWAY

Black

Lower
Norris

Ditch

Chapman's
Plantation

Honey Hill

4

Upper
Norris

A14

FEN

260' Ditch
Bridge

Quy
Water

Quy Mill

HIGH

LOW

5

DITCH

Black
House

ROAD

A1303

Newmarket Road

P+L

A

24 ▼

Prospect

Quy Water
Farm

B

A1303

C

Greenhouse
Farm

Longfield
Farm

N E W M A R K E T

550

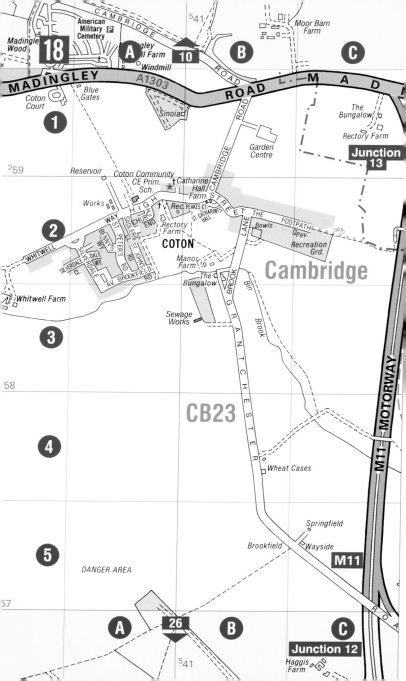

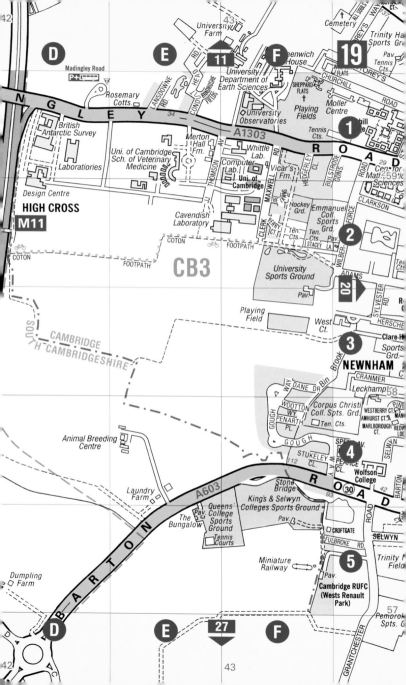

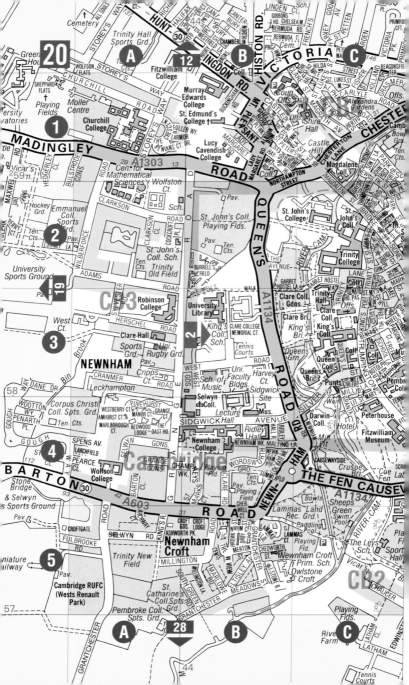

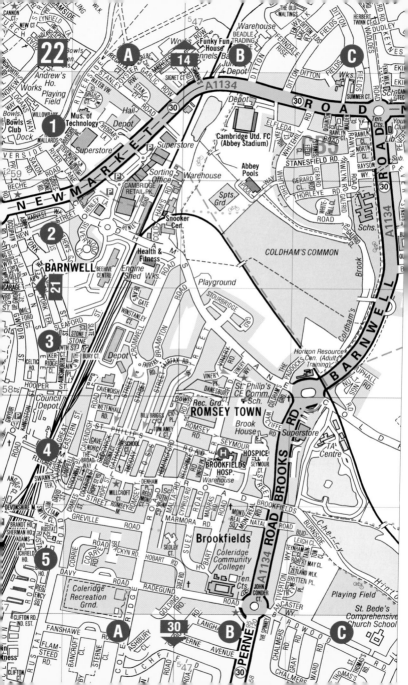

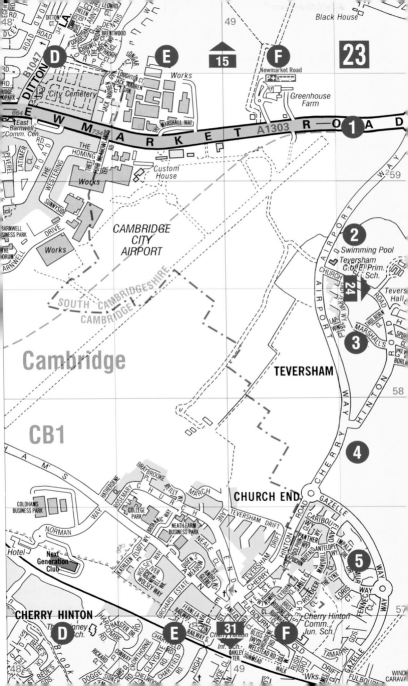

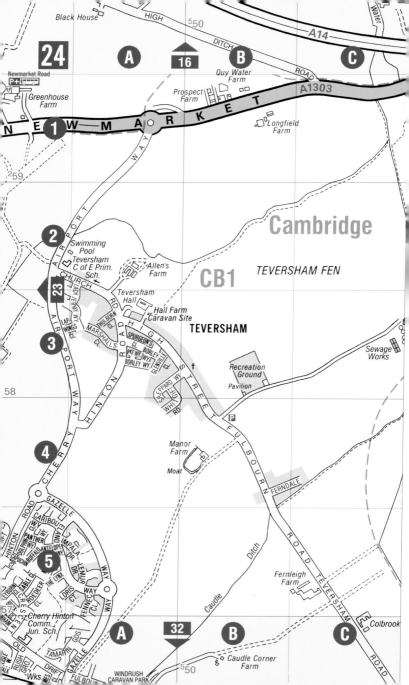

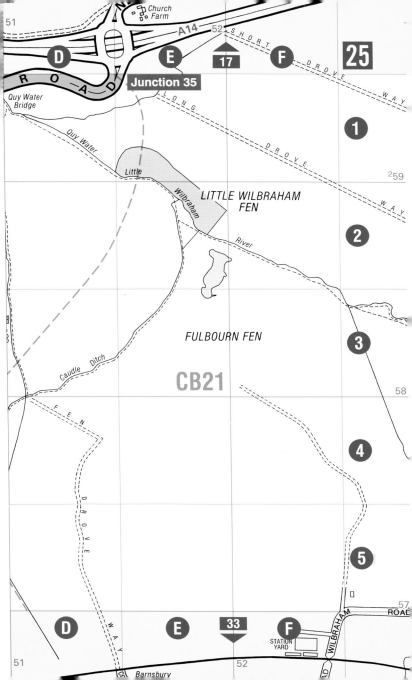

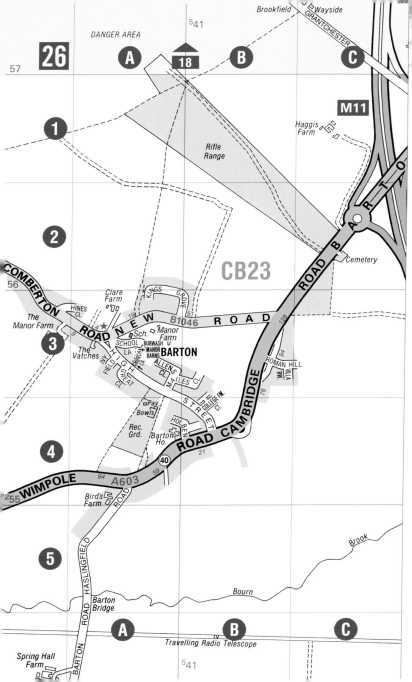

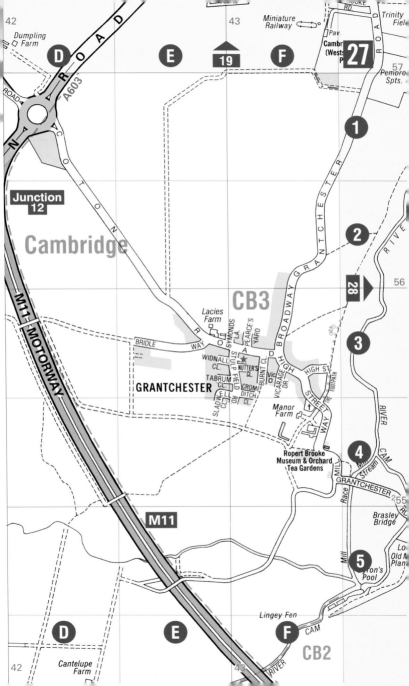

42

Dumpling Farm

D

E

🏠 **19**

F

ROAD

Miniature Railway

Trinity Field

Pav.

Cambr (Wests P.)

27

57 Pembro Spts.

A603

ROAD

BROOKE RD.

ROAD

GRANTCHESTER

1

Junction 12

Cambridge

2

RIVER

COTON

28

56

CB3

BROADWAY

3

Lacies Farm

BRIDLE WAY

ROAD

SYMONDS

PEARCE'S YARD

LA.

WIDNALL CL.

STULP FIELD

NUTTER'S CL.

BURNT CL.

VICARAGE DR.

HIGH ST.

GH

TABRUM CL.

SLAD WELL

FELL RD.

CROME CL.

DITCH CL.

Vic.

THE FOOTPATH

RIVER CAM

GRANTCHESTER

Manor Farm

STREET

WAY

4

Ropert Brooke Museum & Orchard Tea Gardens

GRANTCHESTER

255

RD.

MILL

Race

Stream

Brasley Bridge

M11 MOTORWAY

M11

Mill

5

Byron's Pool

Lo Old N Plan

D

E

Lingey Fen

F

CAM

CB2

42

Cantelupe Farm

43

RIVER

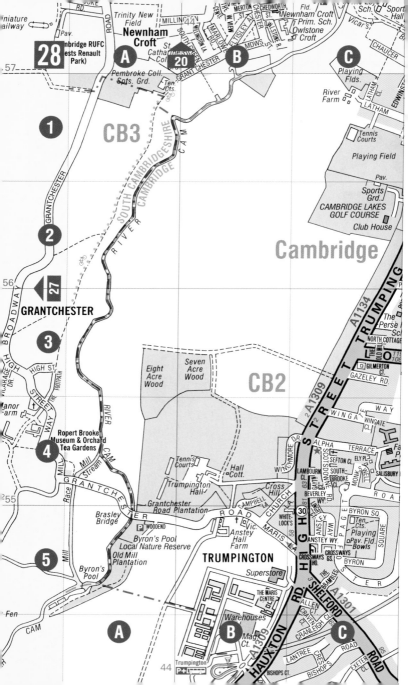

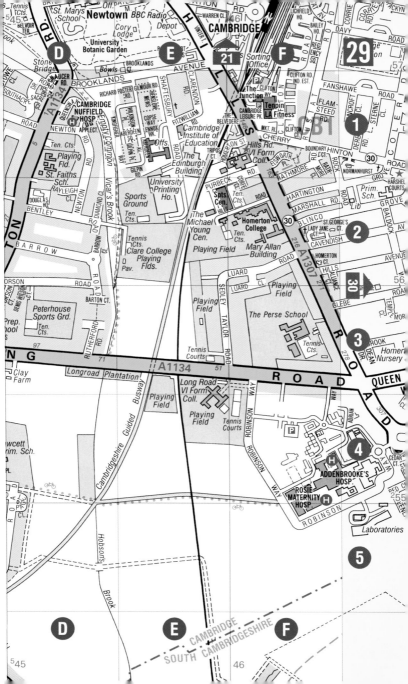

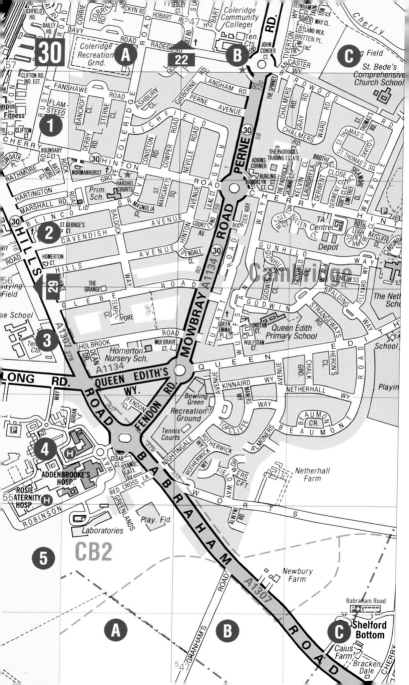

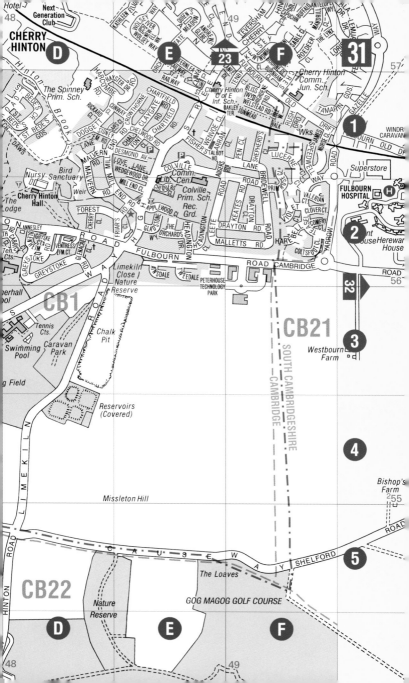

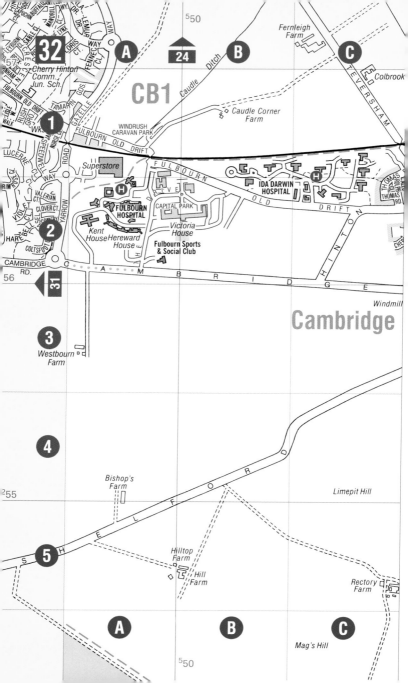

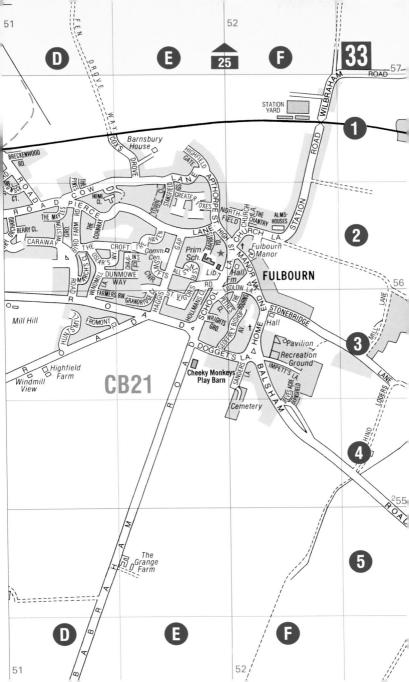

51

52

D **E** ⌂ **25** **F**

57
ROAD

STATION
YARD

1

BRECKENWOOD
RD.

Barnsbury
House

HIGHFIELD
GATE

APTHORPE ST.

LANE

NORTH-
FIELD

CHURCH

THE
CHANTRY

ALMS-
HOUSES

WILBRAHAM ROAD

STATION ROAD

2

56

BERRY CL.

THE MAPLES

WESTON GRO.

THE CORNWAY

GREATER
FOXES

HIGH ST.

CHURCH LA.

Fulbourn
Manor

CARAWA

OSCAR'S WY.

THE
HAVEN

THE
CROFT

Comm.
Cen.

GAP

Prim.
Sch.

★

Lib.

MANOR WK.

FULBOURN

DUNMOWE
WAY

CHAP. INS
CL.

ALL SAINTS

Hall
Fm.

WINDMILL LA.

FARMERS RW.

GRANDRYDGE

HAGGIS

ST. VIGOR'S

HOLLMANS CL.

SCHOOL RD.

LUDLOW
LA.

PETTS

STONEBRIDGE

HOME

MILL LANE

LANE

3

Mill Hill

FROMONT

HUNTSMILL

WRIGHTS GRO.

GEOFFREY BISHOP BROWNS
AV.

Hall

Pavilion

Recreation
Ground

LODERS LANE

HIND LANE

R O A D

Windmill
View

Highfield
Farm

CB21

DOGGET'S LA.

Cheeky Monkeys
Play Barn

SANDERS LA.

IMPETT'S LA.

PETE'S ACRE
BAINSFIELD

BALSHAM

4

Cemetery

255
ROAD

B A B R A H A M   R O A D

The
Grange
Farm

5

51

52

INDEX

Including Streets, Places & Areas, Hospitals etc., Industrial Estates, Selected Flats & Walkways, Stations and Selected Places of Interest.

HOW TO USE THIS INDEX

1. Each street name is followed by its Postcode District, then by its Locality abbreviation(s) and then by its map reference; e.g. **Airport Way** CB1: Tev . . . .2F **23** is in the CB1 Postcode District and the Teversham Locality and is to be found in square 2F on page **23**. The page number is shown in bold type.

2. A strict alphabetical order is followed in which Av., Rd., St., etc. (though abbreviated) are read in full and as part of the street name; e.g. **Brook La.** appears after **Brooklands Ct.** but before **Brooklyn Ct.**

3. Streets and a selection of flats and walkways too small to be shown on the maps, appear in the index with the thoroughfare to which it is connected shown in brackets; e.g. **Adam & Eve Ct.** CB1: Camb . . . .3E **21** (off Adam & Eve St.)

4. Addresses that are in more than one part are referred to as not continuous.

5. Places and areas are shown in the index in BLUE TYPE and the map reference is to the actual map square in which the town centre or area is located and not to the place name shown on the map; e.g. CHERRY HINTON 2E **31**

6. An example of a selected place of interest is Ropert Brooke Mus. & Orchard Tea Gdns. 4F **27**

7. An example of a station is **Cambridge Station (Rail)** . . . .5F **21**, also included is **Park & Ride**, e.g. **Babraham Road (Park & Ride)** 5C **30**

8. An example of a hospital or hospice is ADDENBROOKE'S HOSPITAL 4A **30**

9. Map references for entries that appear on large scale pages **2** & **3** are shown first, with small scale map references shown in brackets; e.g. **Adams Rd.** CB3: Camb 2A **2** (2A **20**)

GENERAL ABBREVIATIONS

Arc. : Arcade		**La.** : Lane	
Av. : Avenue		**Lit.** : Little	
Bus. : Business		**Lwr.** : Lower	
Cvn. : Caravan		**Mnr.** : Manor	
C'way. : Causeway		**Mans.** : Mansions	
Cen. : Centre		**Mdw.** : Meadow	
Chu. : Church		**Mdws.** : Meadows	
Cl. : Close		**M.** : Mews	
Cnr. : Corner		**Mt.** : Mount	
Cotts. : Cottages		**Mus.** : Museum	
Ct. : Court		**Pde.** : Parade	
Cres. : Crescent		**Pk.** : Park	
Cft. : Croft		**Pas.** : Passage	
Dr. : Drive		**Pl.** : Place	
E. : East		**Ri.** : Rise	
Est. : Estate		**Rd.** : Road	
Fld. : Field		**Sq.** : Square	
Flds. : Fields		**St.** : Street	
Gdn. : Garden		**Ter.** : Terrace	
Gdns. : Gardens		**Trad.** : Trading	
Ga. : Gate		**Up.** : Upper	
Gt. : Great		**Vw.** : View	
Grn. : Green		**Vs.** : Villas	
Gro. : Grove		**Vis.** : Visitors	
Ho. : House		**Wlk.** : Walk	
Ind. : Industrial		**Yd.** : Yard	
Info. : Information			

LOCALITY ABBREVIATIONS

Bart : **Barton**	Horn : **Horningsea**
Camb : **Cambridge**	Imp : **Impington**
Che H : **Cherry Hinton**	Land : **Landbeach**
Ches : **Chesterton**	Lit W : **Little Wilbraham**
Cot : **Coton**	Mad : **Madingley**
Fen D : **Fen Ditton**	Milt : **Milton**
Ful : **Fulbourn**	Oak : **Oakington**
Girt : **Girton**	Stow Q : **Stow cum Quy**
Gran : **Grantchester**	Tev : **Teversham**
Gt S : **Great Shelford**	Trum : **Trumpington**
Has : **Haslingfield**	Water : **Waterbeach**
His : **Histon**	

A

Abbey Pools 1B 22	Abbey Wlk. CB1: Camb 2F 21
Abbey Rd. CB5: Camb 1F 21	Abbots Cl. CB4: Camb 2D 13
Abbey Stadium 1B 22	Abbots Way CB25: Horn 5F 9
Abbey St. CB1: Camb 2F 21	Abercorn Pl. CB4: Camb 1D 13
	Aberdeen Av. CB2: Camb 1E 29
	Aberdeen Sq. CB2: Camb 1E 29
	Acrefield Dr. CB4: Camb 1E 21

Acton Way CB4: Camb 4C 12
Adam & Eve Ct. CB1: Camb 3E 21
         (off Adam & Eve St.)
Adam & Eve St. CB1: Camb 3E 21
Adams Ho. CB1: Camb 5F 21
Adams Rd. CB3: Camb 2A 2 (2A 20)
ADC Theatre 1D 3 (2C 20)
ADDENBROOKE'S HOSPITAL 4A 30
Adkins Cnr. CB1: Camb .1B 30
Adrian Way CB2: Camb .4A 30
         (not continuous)
Aingers Rd. CB24: His 2A 6
Ainsdale CB1: Che H 2E 31
Ainsworth Ct. CB1: Camb 3F 21
Ainsworth Pl. CB1: Camb 3A 22
Ainsworth St. CB1: Camb 3F 21
Airport Way CB1: Tev 2F 23
Akeman St. CB4: Camb .4B 12
    CB24: Land 1A 8
Alan Percival Ct. CB4: Ches 5F 13
         (off High St.)
Albemarle Way CB4: Camb 2D 13
Albert Rd. CB25: Stow Q 3F 17
Albert St. CB4: Camb 1D 21
Albion Row CB3: Camb .1B 20
Albion Yd. CB3: Camb 1B 20
         (off Albion Row)
Alder Ct. CB4: Ches 5F 13
Alec Rolph Cl. CB21: Ful 2C 32
Alex Wood Rd. CB4: Camb 3D 13
Alice Bell Cl. CB4: Camb 3F 13
Alice Way CB24: His 1A 6
Allen Ct. CB2: Trum 5C 28
Allens Cl. CB23: Bart 3A 26
Alliance Ct. CB1: Camb .2F 29
Allington Cl. CB24: His 1A 6
All Saint's Pas. CB2: Camb 2D 3 (2C 20)
All Saints Rd. CB21: Ful .2E 33
All Souls La. CB3: Camb 5A 12
Almoners Av. CB1: Camb 4B 30
Almshouses CB21: Ful 2F 33
Alpha Rd. CB4: Camb 1C 20
Alpha Ter. CB2: Trum 4C 28
Alstead Rd. CB24: His 1A 6
Alwyne Rd. CB1: Camb .5B 30
Ambecote CB1: Camb 3E 21
         (off East Rd.)
Ambrose Way CB24: Imp .2B 6
American Military Cemetery 5A 10
Amhurst CB3: Camb 4A 20
Amwell Rd. CB4: Camb .1E 13
Ancaster Way CB1: Camb 5B 22
Anglers Way CB4: Ches .4B 14
Anglia Ruskin University 3F 21
Angus Cl. CB1: Camb 4F 21
Annesley Cl. CB1: Camb 2D 31
Ann's Rd. CB5: Camb 5D 15
Anstey Way CB2: Trum .5C 28
Antelope Way CB1: Che H 5F 23
Apollo Way CB4: Camb .1D 13
Applecourt CB2: Camb .1D 29
Applewood Cl. CB1: Che H 2E 31
Apthorpe St. CB21: Ful .2E 33
Apthorpe Way CB4: Camb 2F 13
Aragon Cl. CB4: Camb 2D 13
Arbury Ct. CB4: Camb 3D 13
ARBURY PARK 1C 12
Arbury Rd. CB4: Camb 2C 12
Arcadia Gdns. CB24: Oak .1B 4
Archway CB3: Camb 5A 20
Arden Rd. CB4: Camb 1E 13
Argyle St. CB1: Camb 4F 21
Armitage Way CB4: Camb 1E 13
Arran Cl. CB1: Che H 1E 31
ARTHUR RANK HOUSE HOSPICE 4B 22
Arthur St. CB4: Camb 5C 12
Arts Picturehouse Cinema 4E 3 (3D 21)
Arts Theatre 3D 3
Arundel Cl. CB4: Camb .4B 12
Ascham Rd. CB4: Camb .5D 13
Ashbury Cl. CB1: Camb .1A 30
Ashcroft Cl. CB4: Camb .2D 13
Ashfield Rd. CB4: Ches .4A 14
Ashley Ct. CB1: Camb 3F 21
         (off Norfolk St.)
Ashvale CB4: Camb 2D 13
Ashworth Pk. CB3: Camb 5A 20

Atherton Cl. CB4: Camb .5E 13
Athlone CB1: Camb 3F 21
         (off Staffordshire St.)
Atkins Cl. CB4: Camb 2F 13
Atrium Club 2F 21
         (off Newmarket Rd.)
Auckland Rd. CB5: Camb 2E 21
Aucklands Cotts. CB5: Camb 2E 21
         (off Auckland Rd.)
Augers Rd. CB1: Che H .1E 31
Augustus Cl. CB4: Camb 1D 13
Australia Cl. CB3: Camb .5A 12
Avenue, The CB3: Camb 2B 2 (2B 20)
    CB23: Mad 2A 10
Aylesborough Cl. CB4: Camb 2C 12
Aylestone Rd. CB4: Camb 1E 21

B

Babraham Rd. CB2: Camb 4A 30
    CB21: Ful 5D 33
    CB22: Camb 4A 30
Babraham Road (Park & Ride) 5C 30
Badminton Cl. CB4: Camb 4B 12
Bagot Pl. CB4: Camb 1E 13
Bailey Ho. CB1: Camb 5F 21
Bailey M. CB5: Camb 2E 21
Bakery Cl. CB5: Fen D 4D 15
Baldock Way CB1: Camb 2A 30
Ballard Cl. CB24: Milt 3C 8
Balsham Rd. CB21: Ful 3F 33
Bancroft Cl. CB1: Camb .1A 30
Bandon Rd. CB3: Girt 3E 11
Banff Cl. CB4: Camb 2D 13
Banhams Cl. CB4: Camb 1E 21
Barnabas Ct. CB24: Milt .5B 8
Barnard Way CB4: Camb 4C 12
Barnes Cl. CB5: Camb 2C 22
Barnsfield CB21: Ful 4F 33
BARNWELL 3F 21
Barnwell Bus. Pk. CB5: Camb 2D 23
Barnwell Dr. CB5: Camb .2D 23
Barnwell Rd. CB5: Camb 3C 22
Barow Cl. CB2: Camb 2D 29
Barrowcrofts CB24: His 1A 6
Barrow Rd. CB2: Camb 2D 29
BARTON 3A 26
Barton Cl. CB3: Camb 4A 20
Barton Rd. CB3: Camb 5D 19
    CB23: Bart 2C 26
    CB23: Has 5A 26
Bassett Cl. CB4: Camb 1E 13
Bateman M. CB2: Camb .5E 21
Bateman St. CB2: Camb .5D 21
Bateson Rd. CB4: Camb .5C 12
Baycliffe Cl. CB1: Camb .2C 30
Bayford Pl. CB4: Camb 1E 13
Beaconsfield Ter. CB4: Camb 5C 12
Beadle Trad. Est. CB5: Camb 5B 14
Beales Way CB4: Camb .2F 13
Beaufort Pl. CB5: Camb 1D 3
Beaulands Cl. CB4: Camb 1E 21
Beaumont Cres. CB1: Camb 4C 30
Beaumont Rd. CB1: Camb 4C 30
Beche Rd. CB5: Camb 2F 21
Beeches, The CB4: Camb 4E 13
Beehive Cen. CB1: Camb 2A 22
Belgrave Rd. CB1: Camb 4B 22
Bell Hill CB24: His 2A 6
Bells Ct. CB3: Camb 1B 20
         (off Castle St.)
Belmont Pl. CB1: Camb 2F 3 (2D 21)
Belmore Cl. CB4: Camb .4B 12
Belvedere, The CB2: Camb 1E 29
Belvoir Rd. CB4: Camb 1E 21
Belvoir Ter. CB2: Camb 5D 21
Benedict Ct. CB24: Milt 4D 9
Benet Cl. CB24: Milt 5B 8
Benet Pl. CB2: Camb 5E 3 (4D 21)
Benet St. CB2: Camb 3D 3 (3C 20)
Benians Ct. CB3: Camb .1A 20
Bennys Way CB23: Cot 2A 18
Benson Pl. CB4: Camb 5B 12
Benson St. CB4: Camb 5B 12
Bentinck St. CB2: Camb .4D 21

Bentinck Ter. CB2: Camb .4D 21
Bentley Rd. CB2: Camb 2D 29
Bergholt Cl. CB5: Camb 5D 15
Bermuda Rd. CB4: Camb .5B 12
Bermuda Ter. CB4: Camb .5B 12
Berrylands CB4: Camb 4E 13
Beverley Way CB2: Trum .4C 28
Biggin La. CB5: Fen D 1E 15
Bill Briggs Ct. CB1: Camb 4A 22
Birch Cl. CB4: Camb 4E 13
Bird Farm Rd. CB21: Ful 2D 33
Birdwood Rd. CB1: Camb .1C 30
Bishops Ct. CB2: Trum 5B 28
Bishop's Rd. CB2: Trum 5C 28
Bishop Way CB24: Imp 3B 6
Blackberry Cl. CB4: Camb 2E 13
Blackhall Rd. CB1: Camb .2B 12
Blackmoor Head Yd. CB5: Camb 1D 3
Blackthorn Cl. CB4: Camb 3E 13
Blackwell Cvn. Site CB4: Camb 5E 7
Blanford Wlk. CB4: Camb .2B 12
Blenheim Cl. CB1: Camb 2D 31
Blinco Gro. CB1: Camb 2F 29
Bliss Way CB1: Che H 1F 31
Blossom St. CB1: Camb 3F 21
Boathouse Ct. CB4: Camb .1D 21
Borley Way CB1: Tev 3A 24
Borrowdale CB4: Camb 3B 12
Bosworth Rd. CB1: Camb .2C 30
Botolph La. CB2: Camb 4D 3 (3C 20)
Boundary Ct. CB1: Camb .1F 29
Bourne Rd. CB4: Ches 4B 14
Bourns, The CB21: Ful 3F 33
Bowers Cft. CB1: Camb 4B 30
Brackenbury CB24: Imp 3B 6
Brackley Cl. CB4: Camb 3C 12
                          (not continuous)
Brackyn Rd. CB1: Camb 5A 22
Bradmore Ct. CB1: Camb .3E 21
                          (off Bradmore St.)
Bradmore La. CB1: Camb .3E 21
Bradmore St. CB1: Camb .3E 21
Bradrushe Flds. CB3: Camb 1E 19
Bradwells Ct. CB1: Camb 3E 3 (3D 21)
Brambles, The CB2: Trum .5C 28
   CB3: Girt 3E 11
Bramley Ct. CB4: Ches 3B 14
Brampton Rd. CB1: Camb .3A 22
Brandon Ct. CB1: Camb 3E 21
                          (off Brandon Pl.)
Brandon Pl. CB1: Camb 3E 21
Brandt Ho. CB1: Camb 5F 21
Bray CB1: Camb 3F 21
                          (off St Matthew's St.)
Braybrooke Pl. CB1: Che H 4E 23
Breckenwood Rd. CB21: Ful 1D 33
Brentwood Cl. CB5: Camb .5D 15
Brentwood Ct. CB5: Camb .5D 15
Bridewell Rd. CB1: Che H .2F 31
Bridgacre CB4: Camb 1E 21
Bridge Rd. CB24: Imp 3B 6
Bridge St. CB2: Camb 1D 3 (2C 20)
Bridgets CB2: Camb 5E 3 (4D 21)
Bridle Way CB3: Gran 3E 27
Brierley Wlk. CB4: Camb 2B 12
Brimley Rd. CB4: Camb 3D 13
Britannic Way CB1: Che H .5E 23
Britten Pl. CB1: Camb 5C 22
Broadmeadows CB4: Camb 1E 21
Broad St. CB1: Camb 3E 21
Broadway CB3: Gran 3F 27
Broadway, The CB1: Camb 4A 22
   CB24: Oak 1B 4
Brook Cl. CB24: His 3A 6
Brookfield Rd. CB23: Cot 2A 18
BROOKFIELDS 5B 22
Brookfields CB1: Camb 4B 22
BROOKFIELDS HOSPITAL .4B 22
Brooklands Av. CB2: Camb 1D 29
Brooklands Ct. CB2: Camb 5E 21
Brook La. CB23: Cot 2B 18
Brooklyn Ct. CB1: Camb 2B 30
Brookmount Ct. CB4: Camb 1E 13
Brookside CB2: Camb 5E 3 (4D 21)
Brookside La. CB2: Camb .5D 21
Brooks Rd. CB1: Camb 4B 22
Brother's Pl. CB1: Camb 1C 30

Brownlow Rd. CB4: Camb .3B 12
Broxbourne Cl. CB1: Che H 5F 23
Brunswick Cotts. CB5: Camb 2E 21
Brunswick Ct. CB21: Ful 2D 33
Brunswick Gdns. CB5: Camb 1F 3 (2E 21)
Brunswick Ter. CB5: Camb 2E 21
Brunswick Wlk. CB5: Camb 1F 3 (2E 21)
Buchan St. CB4: Camb 1D 13
Buckingham Rd. CB3: Camb 1B 20
Budleigh Cl. CB1: Camb 5C 22
Buffalo Way CB1: Che H 5F 23
Bullen Cl. CB1: Camb 2C 30
Bulstrode Gdns. CB3: Camb 1F 19
Bulteel Cl. CB24: Milt 3B 8
Bunker's Hill CB3: Girt 3E 11
Burgess Ho. CB4: Camb 5B 12
                          (off Histon Rd.)
Burgoynes Farm Cl. CB24: Imp 3C 6
Burgoynes Rd. CB24: Imp 3C 6
Burkett Way CB24: His 1A 6
Burleigh Pl. CB1: Camb 2E 21
Burleigh St. CB1: Camb 2E 21
Burling Ct. CB1: Camb 1B 30
Burling Wlk. CB24: Milt 3C 8
Burnham Cl. CB1: Che H 1F 31
Burnside CB1: Camb 5C 22
Burnt Cl. CB3: Gran 3F 27
Burrell's Fld. CB3: Camb 2A 2 (2B 20)
Burrell's Wlk. CB3: Camb 3A 2 (3B 20)
Burrough Fld. CB24: Imp 5B 6
Burwash Mnr. Barns CB23: Bart 3A 26
Bury Ct. CB1: Camb 3A 22
Butcher Cl. CB24: Milt 3B 8
Butler Way CB4: Camb 3C 12
Buttercup Rd. CB4: Camb .2C 12
Butt La. CB24: Milt 3F 7
Byron's Pool Local Nature Reserve 5A 28
Byron Sq. CB2: Trum 5C 28

C

Cadwin Fld. CB4: Camb 2E 13
Caithness Ct. CB4: Camb .1D 13
Caledon Way CB4: Camb .1D 13
Callander Cl. CB4: Camb 2C 12
Cambanks CB4: Ches 5F 13
Camboats 1C 20
CAMBRIDGE 3D 3 (3C 20)
Cambridge & County Folk Mus. 1C 2
Cambridge Bus. Pk. CB4: Camb 2B 14
Cambridge Chesterton Indoor Bowls Club 1F 21
CAMBRIDGE CITY AIRPORT 2E 23
Cambridge City FC 5D 13
Cambridge Contemporary Art 2D 3
Cambridge Golf Driving Range 2B 14
CAMBRIDGE LEA SPIRE HOSPITAL 4B 6
Cambridge Leisure Pk. CB1: Camb 1F 29
CAMBRIDGE NUFFIELD HOSPITAL 1D 29
Cambridge Pl. CB2: Camb .4E 21
Cambridge Retail Pk. CB5: Camb 2A 22
Cambridge Rd. CB3: Girt 5D 5
   CB21: Ful 2F 31
   CB23: Bart 4B 26
   CB23: Mad 5A 10
   CB24: Imp 5B 6
                          (not continuous)
   CB24: Milt 5B 8
   CB24: Oak 1B 4
Cambridge Rd. Ind. Est. CB24: Milt 5B 8
Cambridge RUFC 5F 19
Cambridge Science Pk. CB4: Camb 1F 13
Cambridge Snooker Cen. 2A 22
Cambridge Station (Rail) 5F 21
Cambridge Technopark CB5: Camb 1C 22
Cambridge United FC 1B 22
Cambury Ct. CB4: Camb 1F 13
Cam C'way. CB4: Ches 3A 14
Camden Cl. CB1: Camb 4F 3 (3D 21)
Cameron Rd. CB4: Camb 2D 13
Campbell La. CB2: Trum 4B 28
Campbell St. CB1: Camb 4A 22
Campkin Ct. CB4: Camb 2E 13
Campkin Rd. CB4: Camb 3D 13
Camside CB4: Ches 5F 13
Cannon Cl. CB4: Ches 5F 13
Canterbury Cl. CB4: Camb .5B 12

Canterbury Ct. CB4: Camb 5B 12
Canterbury St. CB4: Camb 5B 12
Capital Pk. CB21: Ful 2A 32
Capstan Cl. CB4: Ches 1F 21
Capuchin Ct. CB1: Che H 5F 23
Caravere Cl. CB4: Camb 1E 13
Caraway Rd. CB21: Ful 2D 33
Caribou Way CB1: Che H 5F 23
Carisbrooke Rd. CB4: Camb 4B 12
Carlow *CB1: Camb* *3F 21*
(off St Matthew's St.)
Carlton Ct. CB4: Camb 4C 12
Carlton Ter. CB4: Camb 4C 12
Carlton Way CB4: Camb 4C 12
Carlyle Rd. CB4: Camb 1C 20
Caroline Pl. CB1: Camb 3E 21
Carrick Cl. CB1: Camb 2D 31
Castle Pk. CB3: Camb 1C 20
Castle Row CB3: Camb 1B 20
Castle St. CB3: Camb 1C 2 (1B 20)
Catharine St. CB1: Camb 4A 22
Causeway Pas. *CB1: Camb* *2E 21*
(off Maid's C'way.)
Causewayside CB3: Camb 5C 2 (4C 20)
Cave Ind. Est. CB4: Camb 3C 14
Cavendish Av. CB1: Camb 2F 29
Cavendish Ct. CB1: Camb 4A 22
Cavendish Pl. CB1: Camb 3A 22
Cavendish Rd. CB1: Camb 4A 22
Cavesson Ct. CB4: Camb 3B 12
Cedar Ct. CB2: Camb 4A 30
Celtic Ho. CB1: Camb 3F 21
Cenacle, The CB3: Camb 5B 20
Central Av. CB4: Camb 1C 12
Central Dr. CB4: Camb 1C 12
Chalfont Cl. CB1: Che H 1E 31
Chalk Gro. CB1: Camb 3C 30
Chalmers Rd. CB1: Camb 1B 30
Chamberlin Ct. CB4: Camb 5B 12
Chambers Dr. CB4: Camb 1D 13
Champneys Wlk. CB3: Camb 5A 2 (4B 20)
Chancellors Wlk. CB4: Camb 3B 12
Chantry, The CB21: Ful 2F 33
Chantry Cl. CB4: Camb 5E 13
Chapel St. CB4: Ches 5F 13
Chaplin's Cl. CB21: Ful 2E 33
Chapman Ct. CB4: Camb 2D 13
Chariot Way CB4: Camb 1C 12
Charles St. CB1: Camb 5A 22
Chartfield Rd. CB1: Che H 1E 31
Chatsworth Av. CB4: Camb 4B 12
Chaucer Cl. CB1: Camb 1D 29
Chaucer Rd. CB2: Camb 5C 20
Chauffeur Punts 4C 2 (3C 20)
Cheddar's La. CB5: Camb 1A 22
Chedworth St. CB3: Camb 5B 20
Cheeky Monkeys Play Barn 3E 33
Chelsea M. CB4: Camb 5B 12
Chelwood Rd. CB1: Che H 1E 31
Cheney Way CB4: Ches 4B 14
Chequers Cl. CB1: Che H 2E 31
Chequers Rd. CB24: Imp 4B 6
Cherry Bounds Rd. CB3: Girt 1D 11
Cherry Cl. CB1: Che H 2D 31
  CB24: Milt 3C 8
CHERRY HINTON 2E 31
Cherry Hinton Hall 2D 31
Cherry Hinton Rd. CB1: Che H, Tev 5F 23
  CB1: Camb 1F 29
  CB22: Camb 5C 30
Cherry Orchard CB21: Ful 2C 32
  CB24: Oak 1B 4
Cherwell Ct. CB3: Camb 5B 20
Chesterfield Rd. CB4: Camb 3F 13
CHESTERTON 5F 13
Chesterton Hall Cres. CB4: Camb 5E 13
Chesterton La. CB4: Camb 1C 2 (1C 20)
Chesterton Mills CB4: Camb 5B 12
Chesterton Rd. CB4: Camb 1C 20
Chesterton Towers *CB4: Ches* *5F 13*
(off Chapel St.)
Chestnut Gro. CB4: Camb 5E 13
Chieftain Way CB4: Camb 1C 12
Chigwell Cl. CB5: Camb 5D 15
Chivers Way CB24: His 4A 6
Christchurch St. CB1: Camb 2E 21
Christ's College Gdns. 2E 3

Christ's Ct. CB1: Camb 3F 3 (3D 21)
Christ's La. CB1: Camb 3E 3 (3D 21)
Christ's Pieces 2F 3 (2D 21)
CHURCH END 5E 23
Church End CB1: Che H 4E 23
  CB23: Cot 2A 18
  CB25: Horn 4F 9
Churchfield Ct. CB3: Girt 4D 5
Churchill Rd. CB3: Camb 1F 19
Church La. CB2: Trum 5B 28
  CB3: Girt 1D 11
  CB21: Ful 2F 33
  CB23: Bart 3A 26
  CB24: Milt 4C 8
Church of St Mary the Great *3D 3*
(off St Mary's St.)
Church Rate Wlk. CB3: Camb 5B 2 (4B 20)
Church Rd. CB1: Tev 2A 24
  CB25: Stow Q 5E 17
Church St. CB4: Ches 5F 13
  CB5: Fen D 4D 15
  CB24: His 1A 6
Church Wlk. CB2: Camb 3E 3
Cineworld
  Cambridge *1F 29*
(off Clifton Rd.)
Circus Dr. CB4: Camb 1C 12
City Ground 5D 13
City Rd. CB1: Camb 3E 21
Clare Bridge 3C 2 (3B 20)
Clare College Gdns. 3B 2 (3B 20)
Clare College Memorial Ct. CB3: Camb 3B 2 (3B 20)
Clare Ct. CB24: Milt 4C 8
Claremont CB2: Camb 5E 21
Clarendon Rd. CB2: Camb 1E 29
Clarendon St. CB1: Camb 3F 3 (3D 21)
Clare Rd. CB3: Camb 4B 20
Clare St. CB4: Camb 5B 12
Clarkson Cl. CB3: Camb 1A 2 (2A 20)
Clarkson Rd. CB3: Camb 1A 2 (2A 20)
Clay Cl. La. CB24: Imp 3C 6
Claygate Rd. CB1: Che H 1E 31
Clayhithe Rd. CB25: Horn 4F 9
Clay St. CB24: His 1A 6
Clerk Maxwell Rd. CB3: Camb 2F 19
Clifton Ct. CB1: Camb 1F 29
Clifton Rd. CB1: Camb 1F 29
Clifton Rd. Ind. Est. CB1: Camb 1F 29
Clifton Way CB1: Camb 1F 29
Cliveden Ct. CB4: Camb 4B 12
Clover Ct. CB1: Che H 2F 31
Coach Ho. Ct. CB4: Camb 5E 13
Cobble Yd. *CB1: Camb* *2E 21*
(off Napier St.)
Cobholm Pl. CB4: Camb 1E 13
Cockburn St. CB1: Camb 4A 22
Cockcroft Pl. CB3: Camb 1A 2 (2A 20)
Cockerell Rd. CB4: Camb 4C 12
Cockerton Rd. CB3: Girt 5D 5
Codon Cl. CB4: Ches 4E 13
Coe's Ct. CB1: Camb 2C 30
Coggeshall Cl. CB5: Camb 5D 15
Coldhams Bus. Pk. CB1: Camb 4D 23
Coldham's Gro. CB1: Camb 4B 22
Coldham's La. CB1: Camb, Che H 2A 22
Coldham's Rd. CB1: Camb 2A 22
Coleridge Rd. CB1: Camb 1A 30
Coles La. CB24: Oak 1B 4
Coles Rd. CB24: Milt 4C 8
College Farm Ct. CB23: Bart 4B 26
College Flds. CB4: Camb 3E 13
College Pk. CB1: Che H 5E 23
College Rd. CB24: Imp 5A 6
Collier Rd. CB1: Camb 3E 21
Colliers La. CB25: Stow Q 3F 17
Coltsfoot Cl. CB1: Che H 2F 31
Colville Rd. CB1: Che H 1E 31
Colwyn Cl. CB4: Camb 4C 12
Comberton Rd. CB23: Bart 2A 26
Comfrey Ct. CB1: Che H 2F 31
Conder Cl. CB24: Milt 3B 8
Conduit Head Rd. CB3: Camb 1E 19
Coniston Rd. CB1: Camb 1A 30
Consul Ct. *CB4: Camb* *1D 13*
(off Apollo Way)
Conway Cl. CB1: Che H 1E 31
Cook Cl. CB4: Ches 3A 14

Cooper Ho. CB4: Camb 5B 12
　　　　　　　　　　　　　　(off Histon Rd.)
Coppice, The CB24: Imp 5B 6
Copse Way CB2: Camb .1E 29
Corfe Cl. CB2: Camb 2F 29
Cambridge Corn Exchange 3D 3
Corn Exchange St. CB2: Camb 3D 3 (3C 20)
Cornway, The CB21: Ful 2D 33
Corona Rd. CB4: Camb .5D 13
Coronation M. CB2: Camb 5D 21
Coronation Pl. CB2: Camb 4D 21
Coronation St. CB2: Camb 5D 21
Corrie Rd. CB1: Camb .5A 22
Cosin Ct. CB2: Camb 5E 3 (4D 21)
COTON 2A 18
Coton Footpath CB3: Camb 2D 19
Coton Rd. CB3: Gran 1D 27
Cottenham Rd. CB24: His 1A 6
Coulson Cl. CB24: Milt 4B 8
Courtland Av. CB1: Camb 2B 30
Courtney Way CB4: Camb 4D 13
Covent Gdn. CB1: Camb 4E 21
Cow La. CB21: Ful 2D 33
Cowley Pk. CB4: Camb .2A 14
Cowley Rd. CB4: Camb .2B 14
Cowley Road (Park & Ride) 2B 14
Cowper Rd. CB1: Camb .1A 30
Cox's Drove CB21: Ful .1E 33
Craister Ct. CB4: Camb .2D 13
Crane Ind. Est. CB24: Milt 5C 8
Cranleigh Cl. CB2: Trum 5C 28
Cranmer Rd. CB3: Camb 4A 2 (3A 20)
Cranwell Ct. CB4: Camb 5B 12
Crathern Way CB4: Camb 2E 13
Craven Cl. CB2: Trum 5C 28
Crawford Cl. CB4: Camb 1D 13
Crescent, The CB3: Camb 1A 20
　　CB24: Imp 5B 6
Crispin Cl. CB4: Camb .2C 12
Crispin Pl. CB1: Camb .2E 21
Croft, The CB21: Ful 2D 33
Croft Cl. CB24: His 1A 6
Croft Gdns. CB3: Camb 5B 20
Croftgate CB3: Camb 5A 20
Croft Holme La. CB4: Camb 1D 21
Croft La. CB24: Oak 1A 4
Croft Lodge CB3: Camb 5B 20
Cromarty Pl. CB4: Camb 4A 22
Crome Ditch Cl. CB3: Gran 3F 27
Cromwell Cl. CB1: Camb 2F 3
Cromwell Rd. CB1: Camb 3A 22
Crosfield Ct. CB4: Camb 2D 13
Cross St. CB1: Camb 4E 21
Crossways Gdns. CB2: Trum 5C 28
Crossways Ho. CB2: Trum 5C 28
Crowland Way CB4: Camb 2E 13
Crowthorne Cl. CB1: Che H 1E 31
Cunningham Ct. CB4: Camb 3D 13
Cutter Ferry Cl. CB4: Camb 1F 21
Cutter Ferry La. CB4: Camb 1E 21
Cutter Ferry Path CB4: Camb 1E 21
Cyprus Rd. CB1: Camb .5B 22

D

Daisy Cl. CB4: Camb 2C 12
Dalegarth CB4: Camb 5E 13
Dalton Sq. CB4: Ches 4A 14
Dane Dr. CB3: Camb 3F 19
Danesbury Ct. CB1: Camb 3B 22
Daniels Ho. CB4: Camb 5B 12
Darwin Dr. CB4: Camb .4B 12
Davey Cl. CB24: Imp 3B 6
Davey Ho. CB4: Ches 4F 13
David Bull Way CB24: Milt 3C 8
David St. CB1: Camb 4F 21
Davy Rd. CB1: Camb 5A 22
Daws Cl. CB1: Che H 1E 31
Daws La. CB1: Che H 1D 31
Days Mdw. CB24: Oak 1B 4
Dean Dr. CB1: Camb 3A 30
Deans Ga. CB1: Camb .3A 22
De Freville Av. CB4: Camb 1E 21
Denham Pl. CB1: Camb .4A 22
Denis Wilson Ct. CB2: Camb 3D 29
Dennis Rd. CB5: Camb .5E 15

Derby Rd. CB1: Camb 1A 30
Derby St. CB3: Camb 5B 20
Derwent Cl. CB1: Camb 2C 30
Desmond Av. CB1: Che H 1E 31
Devonshire Rd. CB1: Camb 5F 21
Devonshire Rd. CB1: Camb 4F 21
Diamond Cl. CB2: Camb 2D 29
Discovery Way CB4: Ches 3B 14
Ditchburn Pl. CB1: Camb 4F 21
Ditton Cl. CB5: Camb 5D 15
Ditton Flds. CB5: Camb 1B 22
Ditton La. CB5: Camb 1D 23
Ditton Wlk. CB5: Camb .5B 14
Dock La. CB25: Horn 4F 9
Doctor's Cl. CB24: Imp 3C 6
Dodford La. CB3: Girt 4C 4
Dogget's La. CB21: Ful .3E 33
Doggett Rd. CB1: Che H 1D 31
Dole, The CB24: Imp 3B 6
　　　　　　　　　　　　　　(not continuous)
Dolphin Cl. CB1: Che H .5F 23
Donegal CB1: Camb 2F 21
　　　　　　　　　　　(off Staffordshire St.)
Douglas Ho. CB2: Camb 2D 29
Dover St. CB1: Camb 3E 21
Dowding Way CB4: Camb 3C 12
Downhams La. CB4: Camb 3E 13
　　　　　　　　　　　　　　(not continuous)
Downing Pl. CB2: Camb 4E 3 (3D 21)
Downing St. CB2: Camb 4E 3 (3D 21)
Drake Way CB24: Imp 2C 6
Drayton Cl. CB1: Che H .2F 31
Drayton Rd. CB1: Che H 2F 31
Drift, The CB24: Oak 1A 4
Drive, The CB21: Ful 2A 32
Drosier Rd. CB1: Camb 5F 3 (4E 21)
Drove Way, The CB25: Stow Q 1D 17
Drummer St. CB1: Camb 3E 3 (3D 21)
Dry Drayton Rd. CB24: Oak 2A 4
Duck End CB3: Girt 1D 11
Dudley Rd. CB5: Camb .5C 14
Dundee Cl. CB4: Ches .4F 13
Dunmow Way CB21: Ful 2D 33
Dunsmore Cl. CB5: Camb 5D 15
Dunstan Ct. CB1: Camb 3B 30
Durnford Way CB4: Camb 4D 13
Dwyer-Joyce Cl. CB2: His 2A 6

E

Eachard Rd. CB3: Camb 4A 12
Earl St. CB1: Camb 3F 3 (3D 21)
Eastfield CB4: Ches 4F 13
East Rd. CB1: Camb 3E 21
Eaton Cl. CB4: Camb 3F 13
Edendale Cl. CB1: Camb 2B 30
Edgecombe CB4: Camb 2E 13
Edinburgh Rd. CB4: Ches 4F 13
Edmund Cl. CB24: Milt 4B 8
Edward St. CB1: Camb .3F 21
Edwinstowe Cl. CB2: Camb 1C 28
Egerton Cl. CB5: Camb .5C 14
Egerton Rd. CB5: Camb 5D 15
Eights Marina, The CB4: Camb 1F 21
Ekin Rd. CB5: Camb 5C 14
Ekin Wlk. CB5: Camb 5C 14
Eland Way CB1: Che H .5F 23
Elder Cl. CB4: Camb 3E 13
Elfleda Rd. CB5: Camb .1B 22
Elizabeth Way CB4: Camb 5E 13
Ellesmere Rd. CB4: Camb 3C 12
Ellis Ho. CB4: Camb 4E 13
Ellison Cl. CB4: Camb 2C 12
Elmfield Cl. CB4: Ches .4F 13
Elmfield Rd. CB4: Ches .4F 13
Elms, The CB24: Milt 4B 8
Elm St. CB1: Camb 2F 3 (2D 21)
Elsworth Pl. CB4: Camb .1F 29
Eltisley Av. CB3: Camb .5B 20
Ely Pl. CB2: Trum 4C 28
Ely Rd. CB24: Milt 4C 8
　　CB25: Water 2D 9
Emery Rd. CB1: Camb .3F 21

Emery St. CB1: Camb 3F 21
Emmanuel College Gdns. 3F 3 (3D 21)
Emmanuel Rd. CB1: Camb 3F 3 (3D 21)
Emmanuel St. CB1: Camb 3E 3 (3D 21)
Emperor Ct. CB4: Camb .2D 13
Enfield CB1: Camb 2F 21
(off St Matthew's St.)
Ennisdale Cl. CB4: Camb 2D 13
Enniskillen Rd. CB4: Ches 4A 14
Epworth Cl. CB1: Camb 2F 3 (2D 21)
Erasmus Cl. CB4: Camb .4C 12
Essex Cl. CB4: Camb 4D 13
Etheldred Ho. CB24: His 1A 6
Evening Ct. CB5: Camb .2E 21
Evergreens CB4: Ches 4A 14
Exeter Cl. CB2: Trum 5C 28

F

Fairbairn Rd. CB4: Ches 4B 14
Fair Ct. CB1: Camb 2F 3 (2E 21)
Fairfax Rd. CB1: Camb .3A 22
Fairsford Pl. CB1: Camb 2F 21
Fair St. CB1: Camb 2F 3 (2E 21)
Fairway CB3: Girt 4D 5
Fallowfield CB4: Ches 4A 14
Fanshawe Rd. CB1: Camb 1F 29
Farmers Row CB21: Ful .3D 33
Farmstead CB24: His 1A 6
Farran CB1: Camb 2F 21
(off St Matthew's St.)
Farringford Cl. CB4: Camb 3B 12
Faulkner Cl. CB24: Milt 4B 8
Fazeley Ho. CB1: Camb .2F 21
(off East Rd.)
Felton St. CB1: Camb 4F 21
Fen Causeway, The CB2: Camb 5C 2 (4C 20)
FEN DITTON 4D 15
Fendon Cl. CB1: Camb .4A 30
Fendon Rd. CB1: Camb .4A 30
Fen Drove Way CB21: Ful 4D 25
Fennec Cl. CB1: Che H .5A 24
Fenners Fitness Suite 4E 21
Fenners Lawn CB1: Camb 4E 21
Fen Rd. CB4: Ches 4B 14
CB24: Milt 4C 8
Fen Vw. Ct. CB4: Ches .4C 14
Ferndale CB1: Tev 4B 24
Ferndale Ri. CB5: Camb .5B 14
Fernlea Cl. CB1: Che H .5E 23
Ferrars Way CB4: Camb 3C 12
Ferry La. CB4: Ches 5A 14
Ferry Path CB4: Camb .1E 21
Field La. CB5: Fen D 2D 15
Field Way CB1: Camb 4B 30
Finch Rd. CB4: Camb 4C 12
Fisher's La. CB1: Che H 1E 31
Fisher St. CB4: Camb 1C 20
Fison Rd. CB5: Camb 5D 15
Fitzgerald Pl. CB4: Ches 5F 13
Fitzroy La. CB1: Camb .2E 21
Fitzroy St. CB1: Camb 2F 3 (2E 21)
Fitzwilliam Mus. 5D 3 (4C 20)
Fitzwilliam Rd. CB2: Camb 1E 29
Fitzwilliam St. CB2: Camb 5E 3 (4C 20)
Flack End CB4: Camb 1D 13
Flamstead Rd. CB1: Camb 1F 29
Fletcher's Ter. CB1: Camb 4F 21
Flower St. CB1: Camb 3F 21
Fontwell Av. CB4: Camb 3B 12
Footpath, The CB3: Gran 3F 27
CB23: Cot 2B 18
Fordwich Cl. CB4: Camb 3C 12
Forest Rd. CB1: Che H .2D 31
Fortescue Rd. CB4: Camb 3D 13
Forum Ct. CB4: Camb 2D 13
Foster Rd. CB2: Trum 5C 28
Fox's Cl. CB24: Milt 4C 8
Francis Ct. CB5: Fen D .4E 15
Francis Darwin Ct. CB4: Camb 4B 12
Francis Pas. CB2: Camb 5D 21
Franks La. CB4: Ches 4A 14
Fraser Rd. CB4: Camb 3F 13
Free School La. CB2: Camb 3D 3 (3C 20)
French's Rd. CB4: Camb 5C 12
Friar's Cl. CB1: Che H 2E 31
Froment Way CB24: Milt .3B 8
Fromont Ct. CB21: Ful 3D 33
FULBOURN 2E 33
FULBOURN HOSPITAL .2A 32
Fulbourn Old Drift CB1: Che H 5F 23
(not continuous)
CB21: Ful 1A 32
Fulbourn Rd. CB1: Che H 2E 31
CB1: Tev 4B 24
Fulbourn Sports & Social Club 2A 32
Fulbrooke Rd. CB3: Camb 5A 20
Fuller Way CB3: Camb .1A 20
Funky Fun House 5B 14

G

Gainsborough Cl. CB4: Ches 3A 14
Gala Bingo
Cambridge 2E 3
Galfrid Cl. CB5: Camb 2C 22
Galfrid Rd. CB5: Camb .2C 22
Garden Ct. CB1: Camb .3E 21
CB24: His 1B 6
Garden Wlk. CB4: Camb 5C 12
CB24: His 1B 6
Garlic Row CB5: Camb .1A 22
Garner Cl. CB24: Milt 3B 8
Garret Hostel La. CB2: Camb 2C 2 (2C 20)
CB3: Camb 3B 2 (2B 20)
Garry Dr. CB4: Camb 2F 13
Gayton Cl. CB2: Trum 4C 28
Gazeley Rd. CB2: Trum .3C 28
Gazelle Way CB1: Che H 4F 23
Geldart St. CB1: Camb .2F 21
Geoffrey Bishop Av. CB21: Ful 3E 33
George IV St. CB2: Camb 5F 3 (4E 21)
George Nuttall Cl. CB4: Camb 3F 13
George Pateman Ct. CB1: Camb 5E 21
Georges Ter. CB4: Camb 5B 12
George St. CB4: Camb 5E 13
Gerard Cl. CB1: Camb 1C 22
Gerard Rd. CB5: Camb .1C 22
Gibbons Ho. CB4: Camb 5B 12
Gifford Pl. CB2: Camb 2D 3 (2C 20)
Gifford's Cl. CB3: Girt 1D 11
Gilbert Cl. CB4: Camb 4B 12
Gilbert Rd. CB4: Camb .4B 12
Gilmerton Ct. CB2: Camb 3C 28
Gilmour Rd. CB2: Camb 1E 29
Gilpin Pl. CB2: Camb 1E 29
Gilpin Rd. CB2: Camb 1E 29
GIRTON 5D 5
Girton Rd. CB3: Girt 1E 11
Gisborne Rd. CB1: Camb 1B 30
Gladeside CB4: Camb 3F 13
Gladstone Way CB1: Che H 2E 31
Glassworks, The 1D 3
Glassworld Stadium 4B 6
Glebe Rd. CB1: Camb 3A 30
Glebe Way CB24: His 2B 6
Glenacre Cl. CB1: Camb 2D 31
Glendale CB24: Milt 5B 8
Glenmere Cl. CB1: Camb 2C 30
Glenmore CB1: Camb 2F 21
(off Staffordshire St.)
Glenoven Ct. CB4: Camb 1C 20
(off Searle St.)
Glenville Cl. CB1: Tev 3A 24
Glisson Rd. CB1: Camb .4E 21
Godesdone Rd. CB5: Camb 2F 21
Goding Way CB24: Milt 4D 9
Godwin Cl. CB1: Camb .3B 30
Godwin Way CB1: Camb 3B 30
Golding Rd. CB1: Camb .5A 22
Gonville Pl. CB1: Camb 5F 3 (4E 21)
Gough Way CB3: Camb .4F 19
Gowers, The CB3: Girt 5D 5
Grafton Cen. CB1: Camb 2E 21
Grafton St. CB1: Camb .2E 21
Graham Rd. CB4: Camb .1D 13
Grand Arc. CB2: Camb 3E 3 (3D 21)
Grandridge Cl. CB21: Ful 3E 33
Grange, The CB1: Camb 2A 30
Grange Cl. CB3: Camb 5A 2 (4A 20)
Grange Dr. CB3: Girt 2D 11
Grange Gdns. CB3: Camb 5A 2 (4A 20)

Grange Rd.—Homefield Cl.

|---|---|
Grange Rd. CB3: Camb	5A 2 (4A 20)
Granham's Rd. CB22: Gt S	5B 30
Granta Pl. CB2: Camb	5C 2 (4C 20)
GRANTCHESTER	3F 27
Grantchester Mdws. CB3: Camb	5B 20
Grantchester Rd. CB2: Trum	4A 28
CB3: Camb	2F 27
CB3: Gran	4A 28
CB23: Cot	3B 18
Grantchester St. CB3: Camb	5B 20
Grasmere Gdns. CB4: Camb	1C 20
Gray Ho. CB4: Ches	4F 13
Grayling Cl. CB4: Ches	5F 13
Gray Rd. CB1: Camb	1C 30
Great Cl. CB23: Bart	3A 26
Gt. Eastern St. CB1: Camb	4F 21
Greater Foxes CB21: Ful	2E 33
Grebe Cl. CB5: Camb	5A 14
Green, The CB4: Ches	4A 14
CB24: His	2A 6
Green End CB5: Fen D	3D 15
Green End Rd. CB4: Ches	3A 14
Greenlands CB2: Camb	4A 30
Greenleas CB24: His	1A 6
Green Pk. CB4: Ches	3A 14
Greens Health & Fitness	
Cambridge	2A 22
Green's Rd. CB4: Camb	5D 13
Green St. CB2: Camb	2D 3 (2C 20)
Gresham Cl. CB1: Camb	5F 3 (4E 21)
Gresham Rd. CB1: Camb	5F 3 (4E 21)
Gretton Ct. CB3: Girt	5C 4
Greville Rd. CB1: Camb	5A 22
Greystoke Ct. CB1: Camb	2D 31
Greystoke Rd. CB1: Camb	2D 31
Grieve Ct. CB4: Ches	4B 14
Grosvenor Ct. CB3: Camb	4A 12
Grove, The CB4: Ches	3A 14
Guest Rd. CB1: Camb	3E 21
Guildhall	
Cambridge	3C 20
(off Wheeler St.)	
Guildhall Pl. CB2: Camb	3D 3
Guildhall St. CB2: Camb	3D 3 (3C 20)
Gunhild Cl. CB1: Camb	2C 30
Gunhild Ct. CB1: Camb	2B 30
Gunhild Way CB1: Camb	2B 30
Gunnell Cl. CB24: Milt	4C 8
Gunning Way CB4: Camb	3C 12
Gun's La. CB24: His	1F 5
Gurney Way CB4: Camb	5D 13
Gwydir St. CB1: Camb	3F 21

H

Hadleigh Ct. CB5: Camb	5D 15
Haggis Gap CB21: Ful	3E 33
Haig Ct. CB4: Ches	5F 13
Hale Av. CB4: Camb	5C 12
Hale St. CB4: Camb	1C 20
Half Acre CB24: Milt	4B 8
Half Moon Yd. CB5: Camb	1D 3
(off Thompson's La.)	
Halifax Rd. CB4: Camb	5A 12
Hall End CB24: Milt	4C 8
Hall Farm Rd. CB4: Camb	4C 12
Hamilton Rd. CB4: Camb	1E 21
Hanover Ct. CB2: Camb	4E 21
(off George IV St.)	
Hanson Ct. CB4: Camb	2D 13
Harcombe Rd. CB1: Che H	1D 31
Harding Way CB4: Camb	3B 12
CB24: His	2A 6
Hardwick St. CB3: Camb	5B 20
Harebell Cl. CB1: Che H	2F 31
Harris Rd. CB4: Camb	3C 12
Harry Scott Ct. CB4: Camb	2D 13
Harshel Courts CB1: Camb	2A 30
Hartington Gro. CB1: Camb	2F 29
Harvest Way CB1: Camb	2F 21
Harvey Goodwin Av. CB4: Camb	5C 12
Harvey Goodwin Ct. CB4: Camb	5C 12
Harvey Goodwin Gdns. CB4: Camb	5C 12
Harvey Rd. CB1: Camb	5F 3 (4E 21)
Haslingfield Rd. CB23: Bart	5A 26
Hatherdene Cl. CB1: Camb	4D 23

Hauxton Rd. CB2: Trum	5B 28
Haven, The CB21: Ful	2E 33
Havenfield CB4: Camb	4E 13
Haviland Way CB4: Camb	3E 13
Hawkins Rd. CB4: Camb	2E 13
Hawthorn Way CB4: Camb	5E 13
Haymarket Rd. CB3: Camb	1B 2 (1B 20)
Hayster Dr. CB1: Che H	1E 31
Haytor CB24: Milt	4B 8
Hazelwood Cl. CB4: Camb	2B 12
Headford Cl. CB5: Camb	5C 14
Headington Cl. CB1: Che H	2E 31
Headington Dr. CB1: Che H	2E 31
Heath Ho. CB4: Ches	4F 13
Hedgerley Cl. CB3: Camb	1F 19
Helen Cl. CB5: Camb	5D 15
Hemingford Rd. CB1: Camb	4A 22
Henley La. CB1: Camb	2A 22
Henley Rd. CB1: Camb	2A 22
Henry Morris Rd. CB4: Imp	3B 6
Henslow M. CB2: Camb	1E 29
Herbert St. CB4: Camb	5D 13
Herbert Twinn Ct. CB5: Camb	5C 14
Hercules Cl. CB4: Camb	1D 13
Hereward Cl. CB24: Imp	3B 6
Heron's Cl. CB4: Camb	3C 30
Herring's Cl. CB25: Stow Q	4F 17
Herschel Rd. CB3: Camb	3A 2 (3A 20)
Hertford St. CB4: Camb	1C 20
Hester Adrian Way CB4: Camb	5E 13
Hick's La. CB3: Girt	1D 11
HIGH CROSS	2D 19
Highdene Rd. CB1: Che H	1F 31
High Ditch Rd. CB5: Fen D	4E 15
Highfield Av. CB4: Camb	4D 13
Highfield Ga. CB21: Ful	1E 33
Highfield Rd. CB24: Imp	5B 6
Highsett CB2: Camb	5E 21
High St. CB1: Che H	2E 31
CB2: Tev	3A 24
CB2: Trum	5C 28
CB3: Girt	5D 5
CB3: Gran	3F 27
CB4: Ches	5F 13
CB5: Fen D	4D 15
CB21: Ful	2E 33
CB23: Bart	3A 26
CB23: Cot	2A 18
CB24: His	2A 6
CB24: Land	1C 8
CB24: Milt	4C 8
CB24: Oak	1B 4
CB25: Horn	5F 9
Highworth Av. CB4: Camb	4E 13
Hilda St. CB4: Camb	5C 12
Hilderstone Ho. CB1: Camb	2F 21
(off Staffordshire St.)	
Hills Av. CB1: Camb	2A 30
Hills Rd. CB2: Camb	5F 3 (4E 21)
(not continuous)	
Hills Road Sports & Tennis Cen.	2E 29
Hind Loders CB21: Ful	4F 33
Hines Cl. CB23: Bart	3A 26
Hinton Av. CB1: Camb	2B 30
Hinton Rd. CB21: Ful	2C 32
HISTON	2A 6
Histon FC	4B 6
Histon Footpath CB3: Girt	4E 5
Histon Rd. CB4: Camb	2B 12
Hoadly Rd. CB3: Camb	4A 12
Hobart Rd. CB1: Camb	5A 22
(not continuous)	
Hobson's Pas. CB1: Camb	2E 3 (2D 21)
Hobson St. CB1: Camb	2E 3 (2D 21)
Holben Cl. CB23: Bart	4A 26
Holbrook Rd. CB1: Camb	3A 30
Holland St. CB4: Camb	1C 20
Hollmans Cl. CB21: Ful	3E 33
Hollymount CB1: Camb	2F 21
(off St Matthew's St.)	
Holme Cl. CB24: Oak	1B 4
Holyoake Ct. CB5: Camb	1B 22
Holyrood Cl. CB4: Camb	3B 12
Home Cl. CB21: Ful	2D 33
CB24: His	3A 6
Home End CB21: Ful	3F 33
Homefield Cl. CB24: Imp	3B 5

Homerton Ct. CB1: Camb 2F 29
Homerton St. CB2: Camb 1E 29
Homing, The CB5: Camb 1D 23
Honey Hill CB3: Camb 1B 2 (1B 20)
Honey Hill M. CB3: Camb 1B 2 (1B 20)
Hooper St. CB1: Camb .3F 21
Hope St. CB1: Camb 4A 22
Hope St. Yd. CB1: Camb 4A 22
Hopkins Cl. CB4: Camb 3F 13
HORNINGSEA 4F 9
Horningsea Rd. CB5: Fen D 4E 15
Howard Cl. CB5: Camb 5C 14
Howard Ct. CB5: Camb 4D 15
Howard Rd. CB5: Camb 5C 14
Howes Pl. CB3: Camb .4F 11
Howgate Rd. CB4: Camb 2B 12
Hulatt Rd. CB1: Camb .3B 30
Humberstone Rd. CB4: Camb 1E 21
Humphreys Rd. CB4: Camb 3D 13
Humphries Way CB24: Milt 4C 8
Huntingdon Rd. CB3: Girt 2D 11
Huntley Cl. CB5: Camb 5D 15
Huntsmill CB21: Ful 3D 33
Hurrell Rd. CB4: Camb 3B 12
Hurst Pk. Av. CB4: Camb 4D 13
Hyde Pk. Cnr. CB2: Camb 5F 3 (4D 21)

I

IDA DARWIN HOSPITAL 2C 32
Impala Dr. CB1: Che H .5A 24
Impett's La. CB21: Ful .3F 33
IMPINGTON 3B 6
Impington La. CB24: Imp 3B 6
Impington Sports Cen. .3B 6
Inceni Way CB4: Camb 2C 12
                                            (not continuous)
Inveran CB1: Camb 2F 21
                                        (off St Matthew's St.)
Inverness Cl. CB4: Ches 4F 13
Iver Cl. CB4: Che H 5E 23
Ivy Fld. CB23: Bart 3A 26
Izaak Walton Way CB4: Ches 4B 14

J

Jackson Rd. CB4: Camb 2F 13
Jack Warren Grn. CB5: Camb 1D 23
James Carlton Cl. CB24: Milt 5B 8
James Nurse Cl. CB1: Che H 1F 31
James St. CB1: Camb .2E 21
Jasmine Cl. CB1: Camb 2B 30
Jedburgh Cl. CB4: Camb 2C 12
Jedburgh Ct. CB4: Camb 2D 13
Jeeves Acre CB21: Ful .3F 33
Jermyn Cl. CB4: Camb 3C 12
Jesus Cl. CB5: Camb 1F 3 (2D 21)
Jesus Green 1D 21
Jesus Green Swimming Pool 1D 21
Jesus La. CB5: Camb 1D 3 (2C 20)
Jesus Ter. CB1: Camb 2F 3 (2E 21)
JJ Thomson Av. CB3: Camb 2E 19
John Clarke Ct. CB4: Camb 4E 13
John Conder Ct. CB1: Camb 5B 22
John St. CB1: Camb 3E 21
Jolley Way CB4: Camb 2E 13
Jordan's Yd. CB5: Camb 1D 3
Junction, The 1F 29

K

Kaldor Ct. CB4: Camb 2D 13
                                            (off Buchan St.)
Kathleen Elliott Way CB1: Che H 5E 23
Kay Hitch Way CB24: His 4A 6
Keates Rd. CB1: Che H 2F 31
Kelsey Cres. CB1: Che H 5F 23
Kelsey Kerridge Sports Cen. 3E 21
Kelvin Cl. CB1: Camb .2C 30
Kendal Ct. CB24: Imp .5B 6
Kendal Way CB4: Camb 3A 14
Kensington Ct. CB5: Camb 1C 22
                                        (off Quainton Cl.)
Ken's Way CB24: Milt .4C 8

Kent Way CB4: Camb .2E 13
                                            (not continuous)
Kerridge Cl. CB1: Camb 3F 21
Kerrys Yd. Cvn. Pk. CB4: Camb 4C 14
Kettles Cl. CB24: Oak 1B 4
Kettles Yd. CB3: Camb 1C 2 (1C 20)
Kettle Yard 1C 2
Keynes St. CB1: Camb .5C 14
Kilmaine Cl. CB4: Camb 1E 13
Kimberley Rd. CB4: Camb 1E 21
Kingfisher Way CB2: Camb 1D 29
King's College Chapel .3C 2
Kings Gro. CB23: Bart .3A 26
KING'S HEDGES 2E 13
Kings Hedges Dr. CB4: Camb 1E 13
Kings Hedges Pool 2D 13
King's Hedges Rd. CB4: Camb 2B 12
                                            (not continuous)
King's Pde. CB2: Camb 3D 3 (3C 20)
King's Rd. CB3: Camb .5A 20
Kingston St. CB1: Camb 4F 21
King St. CB1: Camb 2E 3 (2D 21)
Kingsway CB4: Camb .3C 12
            CB24: His 2A 6
Kinnaird Way CB1: Camb 3B 30
Kinross M. CB4: Ches .4F 13
Kinross Rd. CB4: Ches .4F 13
Kirkby Cl. CB4: Camb .4E 13
Kirkwood Rd. CB4: Camb 1E 13
Knight's Way CB24: Milt 3C 8
                                            (not continuous)

L

Laburnum Cl. CB4: Camb 5E 13
Lady Jane Ct. CB1: Camb 2F 29
Lady Jermy Way CB1: Tev 3A 24
Lady Margaret Rd. CB3: Camb 1B 2 (1B 20)
LA Fitness
            Cambridge 1F 29
Lambourn Cl. CB2: Trum 4C 28
Lammas Ct. CB3: Camb 5B 20
Lammas Fld. CB3: Camb 5B 20
LANDBEACH 1C 8
Landbeach Rd. CB24: Milt 1C 8
                                            (not continuous)
Lander Cl. CB24: Milt 3B 8
Langdale Cl. CB1: Che H 5F 23
Langham Rd. CB1: Camb 1B 30
Lansdowne Rd. CB3: Camb 1E 19
Lantree Cres. CB2: Trum 5C 28
Lapwings Cl. CB1: Tev .3F 23
Larchfield CB3: Camb .4A 20
Larkin Cl. CB4: Camb .3F 13
Larmor Dr. CB3: Camb 1A 20
Latham Cl. CB2: Camb 1C 28
Latham Rd. CB2: Camb 1C 28
Latimer Cl. CB5: Camb 1D 23
Laundress La. CB2: Camb 4C 2 (3C 20)
Laundry La. CB1: Camb 2C 30
Lauriston Pl. CB4: Camb 1D 13
Lavender Rd. CB4: Camb 2F 13
Lawns, The CB3: Camb 2F 13
Lawrence Cl. CB3: Girt .1D 11
Lawrence Way CB4: Camb 2E 13
Lawson Cl. CB24: His 2A 6
Laxton Way CB4: Ches .3B 14
Lea Ct. CB24: Milt 4C 8
Lees Way CB3: Girt 5D 5
Leete Rd. CB1: Che H .2E 31
Legate Wlk. CB4: Camb 2D 13
                                        (off Northfields Av.)
Legion Cl. CB4: Camb .2D 13
Lemur Dr. CB1: Che H .5A 24
Lennox Wlk. CB1: Camb 1E 29
Lensfield Rd. CB2: Camb 5E 3 (4D 21)
Lents Way CB4: Ches .4B 14
Leonard Cl. CB5: Camb 5D 15
Lexington Cl. CB4: Camb 4B 12
Leyburn Cl. CB1: Che H 5F 23
Leys Av. CB4: Camb 3D 13
Leys Rd. CB4: Camb 4E 13
Lichfield Ho. CB1: Camb 5F 21
Lichfield Rd. CB1: Camb 1A 30
Lilac Ct. CB1: Camb 2B 30
Lilley Cl. CB4: Ches 4A 14

Limekiln Close Nature Reserve .2E 31
Limekiln Rd. CB1: Camb .4D **31**
Limetree Cl. CB1: Camb .2C **30**
Linden Cl. CB4: Camb .5B **12**
Lingholme Cl. CB4: Camb .4B **12**
Lingrey Ct. CB2: Trum .5C **28**
Lion Yd. CB2: Camb .3E **3**
Lisa Ct. CB4: Ches .4A **14**
Lisle Wlk. CB1: Che H .1F **31**
Lit. St Mary's La. CB2: Camb .5D **3** (4C **20**)
Livermore Cl. CB4: Camb .2E **13**
Llandaff Chambers CB2: Camb .4E **3**
Logans Way CB4: Ches .1F **21**
Lone Tree Av. CB24: Imp .1B **12**
Lone Tree Gro. CB24: Imp .1B **12**
Long Drove Way CB21: Lit W .1E **25**
Long Reach Rd. CB4: Ches .4B **14**
Long Rd. CB2: Camb .3C **28**
Longstanton Rd. CB24: Oak .1A **4**
Longworth Av. CB4: Ches .5F **13**
Loris Ct. CB1: Che H .5A **24**
Loughton Ct. CB5: Camb .1E **23**
Love La. CB1: Che H .1E **31**
Lovell Rd. CB4: Camb .2F **13**
Love's Cl. CB24: His .4B **6**
Lowbury Cres. CB24: Oak .1A **4**
Lwr. Park St. CB5: Camb .1D **3** (2C **20**)
Low Fen Droveway CB5: Fen D .1F **15**
Luard Cl. CB2: Camb .3F **29**
Luard Rd. CB2: Camb .2F **29**
Lucerne Cl. CB1: Che H .1F **31**
Lucketts Cl. CB24: His .1A **6**
Ludlow La. CB21: Ful .2F **33**
Lyndewode Rd. CB1: Camb .4E **21**
Lyndhurst Cl. CB24: Milt .4B **8**
Lynfield La. CB4: Ches .5F **13**
Lynx, The CB1: Che H .5F **23**

M

Macfarlane Cl. CB24: Imp .4B **6**
Mackenzie Rd. CB1: Camb .3F **21**
Madingley Rd. CB3: Camb .1A **2** (1C **18**)
CB23: Cot .1A **18**
Madingley Road (Park & Ride) .1D **19**
Madras Rd. CB1: Camb .5B **22**
Magdalene St. CB3: Camb .1C **2** (1C **20**)
Magnolia Cl. CB1: Camb .2A **30**
Magrath Av. CB4: Camb .1C **20**
Maid's C'way. CB5: Camb .1F **3** (2E **21**)
Mailes Cl. CB23: Bart .3A **26**
Main St. CB25: Stow Q .4F **17**
Maio Rd. CB4: Camb .3E **13**
Maitland Av. CB4: Ches .3A **14**
Maitland Ho. *CB3: Camb .5B 20*
(off Barton Rd.)
Malcolm Pl. CB1: Camb .2E **3** (2D **21**)
Malcolm St. CB1: Camb .1E **3** (2D **21**)
Malden Cl. CB5: Camb .1C **22**
Mallards, The CB5: Camb .1F **21**
Malletts Rd. CB1: Che H .2F **31**
Malta Rd. CB1: Camb .4A **22**
Malting La. CB3: Camb .5B **2** (4B **20**)
Maltings Yd. CB5: Camb .1D **3**
Maltster's Way CB4: Ches .5F **13**
Malvern Rd. CB1: Che H .1D **31**
Mander Way CB1: Camb .2B **30**
Mandrill Cl. CB1: Che H .5F **23**
Maners Way CB1: Camb .3B **30**
Manhatten Dr. CB4: Camb .1E **21**
Manor Ct. CB3: Camb .4A **20**
Mnr. Farm Cl. CB24: Oak .1B **4**
Mnr. Farm Rd. CB3: Girt .4D **5**
Manor Pk. CB24: His .2F **5**
Manor Pl. CB1: Camb .2E **3** (2D **21**)
Manor St. CB1: Camb .2E **3** (2D **21**)
Manor Wlk. CB21: Ful .2F **33**
Mansel Ct. CB4: Camb .3D **13**
Mansel Way CB4: Camb .3D **13**
Mansfield Cl. CB24: Milt .4B **8**
Mansfield Ct. CB4: Ches .5F **13**
Maple Cl. CB4: Camb .4E **13**
Maples, The CB21: Ful .2D **33**
March La. CB1: Che H .4E **23**
March's Cl. CB21: Ful .2D **33**
Marfield Ct. CB4: Camb .4E **13**
Mariner's Way CB4: Ches .1F **21**
Marion Cl. CB3: Camb .5A **12**
Maris Cen., The CB2: Trum .5B **28**
Maris La. CB2: Trum .5B **28**
Market Hill CB2: Camb .3D **3** (3C **20**)
Market Pas. CB2: Camb .2D **3** (2C **20**)
Market Ri. CB1: Camb .1F **29**
Market St. CB2: Camb .2D **3** (2C **20**)
Markham Cl. CB4: Camb .2F **13**
Marks Way CB3: Girt .5D **5**
Marlborough Ct. CB3: Camb .4A **20**
Marlowe Rd. CB3: Camb .5B **20**
Marmora Rd. CB1: Camb .5B **22**
Marshall Rd. CB1: Camb .2F **29**
Marshall's Cl. CB1: Tev .3A **24**
Marshall Way, The CB5: Camb .1E **23**
Martingale Cl. CB4: Camb .3B **12**
Martin's Stile La. CB4: Ches .5F **13**
Masters Ho. CB4: Camb .4B **12**
Mawson Pl. *CB1: Camb .4E 21*
(off Mawson Rd.)
Mawson Rd. CB1: Camb .4E **21**
Mayfield Rd. CB3: Girt .1E **11**
Mayflower Ho. CB4: Camb .1E **21**
Mays Way CB4: Ches .4B **14**
Meadow Cft. *CB4: Ches .5F 13*
(off Lynfield La.)
Meadow Farm Cl. CB24: Oak .1C **4**
Meadowlands Rd. CB5: Camb .1D **23**
Mead Vw. CB24: Oak .1A **4**
Melbourne Pl. CB1: Camb .3F **3** (3E **21**)
Melvin Way CB24: His .2F **5**
Mercers Row CB5: Camb .5A **14**
Mere Way CB4: Camb .3D **13**
CB24: Milt .5E **7**
Merton Rd. CB24: His .3A **6**
Merton St. CB3: Camb .5B **20**
Metcalfe Rd. CB4: Camb .4C **12**
Michaelmas Pl. CB4: Camb .5C **12**
Michaels Cl. CB3: Girt .5D **5**
Mickey Flynn's American Pool Hall *.4F 21*
(off Mill Rd.)
Midhurst Cl. CB4: Ches .5A **14**
Midsummer Common .1E 21
Midsummer Ct. CB4: Camb .1E **21**
Midwinter Pl. CB4: Camb .5E **13**
Milford St. CB1: Camb .3F **21**
Millcroft Ct. CB1: Camb .4A **22**
Mill End Cl. CB1: Che H .2E **31**
Mill End Rd. CB1: Che H .1D **31**
Millers Yd. CB2: Camb .4D **3** (3C **20**)
Millington La. CB3: Camb .5B **20**
Millington Rd. CB3: Camb .5A **20**
Mill La. CB2: Camb .4C **2** (3C **20**)
CB21: Ful .3F **33**
CB24: His .2B **6**
Mill Rd. CB1: Camb .3E **21**
CB24: Imp .5A **6**
Mill St. CB1: Camb .4F **21**
Mill Way CB3: Gran .4F **27**
MILTON .4C **8**
Milton Country Pk. .5C 8
Milton Country Pk. Vis. Cen. .5C 8
Milton Ct. CB24: Milt .4C **8**
MILTON HOSPICE (EAST ANGLIA'S CHILDRENS HOSPICES) .4D 9
Milton Maize Maze, The .2B 8
Milton Rd. CB4: Camb .5D **13**
CB24: Imp .3C **6**
Miltons Wlk. CB1: Camb .2E **3** (2D **21**)
Minerva Way CB4: Camb .1D **13**
Minter Cl. CB25: Stow Q .4F **17**
Missleton Ct. CB1: Camb .2B **30**
Misty Mdws. CB5: Camb .4C **14**
Molewood Cl. CB4: Camb .3B **12**
Moncrieff Cl. CB4: Camb .2D **13**
Monkswell CB2: Trum .4C **28**
Montague Rd. CB4: Camb .5E **13**
Montfort Way CB4: Camb .3D **13**
Montgomery Rd. CB4: Camb .3D **13**
Montreal Rd. CB1: Camb .5B **22**
Montreal Sq. CB1: Camb .5B **22**
Montrose Cl. CB4: Camb .2D **13**
Montrose Ho. CB4: Ches .4F **13**
Moore Cl. CB4: Camb .3F **13**
Mortimer Rd. CB1: Camb .3E **21**
Mortlock Av. CB4: Ches .3A **14**

Moss Bank CB4: Ches 4B 14
Mt. Pleasant CB3: Camb 1B 20
Mt. Pleasant Wlk. CB3: Camb 1B 20
Mowbray Rd. CB1: Camb 3B 30
Mowlam Cl. CB24: Imp 4B 6
Moyne Cl. CB4: Camb 2D 13
Mulberry Cl. CB4: Camb 4E 13
Mulgrave Cl. CB4: Camb 3A 30
Mumford Theatre 3E 21
Muncey Wlk. CB24: His 1A 6
Mus. of Archaeology & Anthropology 4E 3 (3D 21)
Mus. of Classical Archaeology 5B 2 (4B 20)
Mus. of Technology 1A 22
Mus. of Zoology 4E 3 (3C 20)
Musgrave Way CB5: Fen D 3E 15

N

Napier St. CB1: Camb 2E 21
Narrow Cl. CB24: His 1B 6
Narrow La. CB24: His 2A 6
Natal Rd. CB1: Camb 5B 22
Neal Dr. CB4: Camb 1D 13
Neale Cl. CB1: Che H 5E 23
Neath Farm Bus. Pk. CB1: Che H 5E 23
Nelson Cl. CB1: Camb 2F 21
Neptune Cl. CB4: Camb 2D 13
Netherhall Way CB1: Camb 3C 30
Neville Rd. CB1: Camb 1B 30
NEW CHESTERTON 5C 12
New Ct. CB4: Ches 5F 13
Newell Wlk. CB1: Che H 5E 23
Newmarket Rd. CB1: Tev .1D 23
    CB5: Camb 2E 21
    CB25: Stow Q 5E 17
Newmarket Road (Park & Ride) 1F 23
NEWNHAM 4B 20
NEWNHAM CROFT 5B 20
Newnham Cft. St. CB3: Camb 5B 20
Newnham Path CB3: Camb 5B 2 (4B 20)
Newnham Rd. CB3: Camb 5B 2 (4B 20)
Newnham Ter. CB3: Camb 5C 2 (4C 20)
Newnham Wlk. CB3: Camb 5B 2 (4B 20)
New Pk. St. CB5: Camb 1D 3 (1C 20)
New Rd. CB23: Bart 3A 26
    CB24: Imp 4B 6
    CB24: Oak 3D 5
New School Rd. CB24: His .3A 6
New Sq. CB1: Camb 2F 3 (2E 21)
New St. CB1: Camb 2F 21
Newton Rd. CB2: Camb 1D 29
NEWTOWN 5D 21
Next Generation Club
    Cambridge 5D 23
Nicholson Way CB4: Camb 3D 13
Nightingale Av. CB1: Camb 4A 30
Norfolk St. CB1: Camb 3F 21
Norfolk Ter. CB1: Camb 3F 21
Normanhurst CB1: Camb .1A 30
Normanton Way CB24: His .1A 6
Norman Way CB1: Camb .5D 23
Northampton St. CB3: Camb 1B 2 (1B 20)
North Cotts. CB2: Camb 3C 28
Northfield CB3: Girt 4D 5
    CB21: Ful 2F 33
Northfields Av. CB4: Camb 2D 13
North St. CB4: Camb 5B 12
North Ter. CB5: Camb 1F 3 (2E 21)
Northumberland Cl. CB4: Camb 3D 13
Norton Cl. CB5: Camb 1C 22
Norwich St. CB2: Camb 5D 21
Nuffield Cl. CB4: Ches 2B 14
Nuffield Rd. CB4: Ches 2A 14
Nun's Orchard CB24: His 1A 6
Nuns Way CB4: Camb 2E 13
Nursery Wlk. CB4: Camb .4B 12
Nutter's Cl. CB3: Gran 3F 27
Nuttings Rd. CB1: Camb .3C 22

O

OAKINGTON 1B 4
Oakington Rd. CB3: Girt 3D 5
Oakley Ter. CB1: Che H 1F 31
Oaks, The CB24: Milt 4B 8

Oak Tree Av. CB4: Camb 5E 13
Oak Tree Way CB24: His 3A 6
Oast Ho., The CB3: Camb 5A 2 (4A 20)
Oates Way CB24: His 1A 6
Occupation Rd. CB1: Camb 2F 21
Old Farm Cl. CB24: His 1A 6
Old Maltings, The CB5: Camb 5B 14
Old Mill, The CB2: Camb 3C 28
Old St Pauls CB2: Camb 5E 21
Old School La. CB24: Milt 4C 8
Ongar Ct. CB5: Camb 5E 15
Orchard Av. CB4: Camb 4D 13
Orchard Cl. CB3: Girt 5D 5
Orchard Dr. CB3: Girt 2D 11
Orchard End CB24: Milt 5B 8
Orchard Est. CB1: Che H 5E 23
Orchard Rd. CB24: His 1B 6
Orchards, The CB1: Che H 2E 31
Orchard St. CB1: Camb 2F 3 (2D 21)
    CB25: Stow Q 4E 17
Orchard Way CB24: Oak 1B 4
Orwell Furlong CB4: Camb 2B 14
Oslar's Way CB21: Ful 2D 33
Owlstone Rd. CB3: Camb .5B 20
Oxford Rd. CB4: Camb 5A 12
Oyster Row CB5: Camb 1A 22

P

Paddock Cl. CB24: Imp 2B 6
Paddocks, The CB1: Camb 2B 30
                                    (Cherry Hinton Rd.)
    CB1: Camb 3B 22
                                    (Coldham's La.)
Paddocks Trad. Est., The CB1: Camb 1B 30
Pages Cl. CB24: His 2A 6
Paget Cl. CB2: Trum 5D 29
Paget Rd. CB2: Trum 5C 28
Pakenham Cl. CB4: Ches .4F 13
Palmers Wlk. CB1: Camb .3E 21
Pamplin Ct. CB1: Che H 1E 31
Panther Way CB1: Che H .5F 23
Panton St. CB2: Camb 5F 3 (4D 21)
Paradise St. CB1: Camb 2E 21
Park & Ride
    Babraham Road 5C 30
    Cowley Road 2B 14
    Madingley Road 1D 19
    Newmarket Road 1F 23
    Trumpington 5B 28
Park Av. CB24: His 2F 5
Park Dr. CB24: Imp 3B 6
Parker's Piece 4F 3 (3E 21)
Parker's Ter. CB1: Camb 2F 21
Parker St. CB1: Camb 3F 3 (3D 21)
Park La. CB24: His 2E 5
Park Pde. CB5: Camb 1D 3 (1C 20)
Parkside CB1: Camb 3F 3 (3E 21)
Parkside Pool 3E 21
Park St. CB5: Camb 1D 3 (2C 20)
Park Ter. CB1: Camb 4F 3 (3D 21)
Parlour Cl. CB24: His 1A 6
Parr Cl. CB24: Imp 3B 6
Parsonage St. CB5: Camb 2E 21
Parsons Ct. CB2: Camb 3D 3 (3C 20)
Pavilion Ct. CB4: Camb 1D 13
                                    (off Apollo Way)
Peacock Way CB24: His 1A 6
Peakes Ct. CB23: Cot 2B 18
Pearce Cl. CB3: Camb 4A 20
Pearce's Yd. CB3: Gran 3F 27
Pearl Cl. CB4: Ches 5F 13
Pearmain Ct. CB4: Camb .4B 14
Pearson Cl. CB24: Milt 5C 8
Pearson Ct. CB24: Milt 5C 8
Pease Way CB24: His 2E 5
Peas Hill CB2: Camb 3D 3 (3C 20)
Pelham Ct. CB4: Camb 3B 12
Pemberton Cl. CB2: Camb 4D 21
Pemberton Ter. CB2: Camb 4D 21
Pembroke Cl. CB24: Milt 4C 8
Pembroke St. CB2: Camb 4D 3 (3C 20)
Pembroke Way CB1: Tev 3A 24
Penarth Pl. CB3: Camb 4F 19
Pen Cl. CB1: Che H 1F 31
Pentland Pl. CB4: Camb 4C 12

Pentlands Cl. CB4: Camb 1E 21
Pentlands Cl. CB4: Camb 1E 21
Pepys Ct. CB4: Ches 5F 13
Pepys Ter. CB24: Imp 5B 6
Pepys Way CB3: Girt 1D 11
Percheron Cl. CB24: Imp 3C 6
Perne Av. CB1: Camb 1B 30
Perne Rd. CB1: Camb 1B 30
Perowne St. CB1: Camb 4F 21
Perry Ct. CB3: Camb 2F 19
Perse Almshouses CB3: Camb 5B 2
Perse Way CB4: Camb 3C 12
Peter Goodin Cl. CB24: Milt 4B 8
Peterhouse M. CB4: Ches 4A 14
Peterhouse Technology Pk. CB1: Che H 2E 31
Peter Maitland Ct. CB4: Camb 5C 12
Petersfield *CB1: Camb* *3E 21*
(off East Rd.)
Petersfield Mans. CB1: Camb 3E 21
Pettit's Cl. CB21: Ful 3E 33
Petty Cury CB2: Camb 3D 3 (3C 20)
Petworth St. CB1: Camb 2F 21
Peveril Cl. CB5: Camb 1D 23
Peveril Rd. CB5: Camb 1C 22
Pierce La. CB21: Ful 2D 33
Pikes Wlk. CB1: Camb 2F 3 (2D 21)
Pine Ct. CB24: Imp 4B 6
Pinehurst CB3: Camb 5A 2 (4A 20)
Pines, The CB21: Ful 2D 33
Pioneer Ct. CB24: His 4A 6
Pippin Dr. CB4: Ches 3B 14
Plum Tree Cl. CB4: Camb 2B 12
Pool Way CB5: Camb 2B 22
Poplar Rd. CB24: His 3A 6
Porson Ct. CB2: Camb 3D 29
Porson Rd. CB2: Camb 2D 29
Portico Wlk. CB4: Camb 1D 13
Portland Pl. CB1: Camb 2F 3 (2E 21)
Portugal Pl. CB5: Camb 1D 3 (2C 20)
Portugal St. CB5: Camb 1D 3 (2C 20)
(not continuous)
Post Office Ter. CB2: Camb 3E 3 (3D 21)
Pound Hill CB3: Camb 1B 2 (1B 20)
Pretoria Rd. CB4: Camb 1E 21
Primary Ct. CB4: Ches 4A 14
Primrose Cl. CB1: Che H 2F 31
Primrose Cft. CB4: Camb 5C 12
Primrose St. CB4: Camb 5C 12
Prince Andrew Ct. *CB4: Ches* *5A 14*
(off High St.)
Prince Henry Ct. *CB4: Camb* *5B 12*
(off Histon Rd.)
Princess Ct. *CB2: Camb* *4D 21*
(off Bentinck St.)
Prince William Ct. CB4: Camb 5B 12
Prior's Cl. CB24: His 2A 6
Priory Rd. CB5: Camb 1F 21
CB25: Horn 5F 9
Priory St. CB4: Camb 5B 12
Prospect Row CB1: Camb 3F 3 (3E 21)
Pryor Cl. CB24: Milt 4C 8
Purbeck Rd. CB2: Camb 2E 29
Pye Ter. CB4: Ches 5F 13

Q

Quainton Cl. CB5: Camb 1C 22
Quayside CB5: Camb 1C 2 (2C 20)
Queen Ann Ter. *CB1: Camb* *3E 21*
(off Gonville Pl.)
Queen Edith's Way CB1: Camb 3A 30
Queen Emma Pl. CB1: Camb 3B 30
Queens Bridge 4C 2 (3C 20)
Queens' La. CB2: Camb 4C 2 (3C 20)
Queen's Mdw. CB1: Che H 5E 23
Queen's Rd. CB3: Camb 1B 2 (2B 20)
Queens Way CB24: Oak 1C 4
Queensway CB2: Camb 1D 29
Quorum, The CB5: Camb 2D 23
Quy Rd. CB25: Stow Q 2F 17

R

Rachel Cl. CB5: Camb 5D 15
Rackham Cl. CB4: Camb 5B 12

Radegund Rd. CB1: Camb 5A 22
Railway St. CB1: Che H 5E 23
Ramsden Sq. CB4: Camb 2F 13
Ransome Cl. CB4: Ches 5F 13
Rathmore Cl. CB1: Camb 1F 29
Rathmore Rd. CB1: Camb 1F 29
Ravensworth Gdns. CB1: Camb 5F 21
Rawlyn Cl. CB5: Camb 1C 22
Rawlyn Ct. CB5: Camb 1C 22
Rawlyn Rd. CB5: Camb 1C 22
Rayleigh Cl. CB2: Camb 2D 29
Rayson Way CB5: Camb 1C 22
Recreation Cl. CB24: Milt 5C 8
Rectory Ter. *CB1: Che H* *1E 31*
(off High St.)
Red Cross La. CB2: Camb 4A 30
Redfern Cl. CB4: Camb 3D 13
Redgate Rd. CB3: Girt 5D 5
Redmond Ct. CB1: Camb 4A 22
Redwood Lodge CB3: Camb 4A 20
Regatta Cl. CB5: Camb 5A 14
Regency Sq. CB1: Camb 5F 21
Regent St. CB2: Camb 4F 3 (3D 21)
Regent Ter. CB2: Camb 4F 3 (3D 21)
Reilly Way CB1: Che H 4E 23
Rexbury Ct. CB1: Camb 2F 21
Ribston Way CB4: Ches 3B 14
Richard Foster Rd. CB2: Camb 1E 29
Richmond Rd. CB4: Camb 5A 12
Richmond Ter. CB4: Camb 1D 3
Rickard Cl. CB1: Che H 1D 31
Ridley Hall Rd. CB3: Camb 5B 2 (4B 20)
Ring Fort Rd. CB4: Camb 2B 12
Rivar Pl. CB1: Camb 3F 21
River Ct. CB4: Ches 5A 14
River La. CB5: Camb 1F 21
Riverside CB5: Camb 1F 21
Riverside Ct. CB4: Camb 1D 21
Riverside Pl. CB5: Camb 1F 21
Robert Davies Ct. CB4: Ches 2A 14
Robert Jennings Cl. CB4: Camb 3F 13
Robert May Cl. CB1: Camb 5C 22
Robinson Way CB2: Camb 4F 29
Rock Rd. CB1: Camb 1F 29
Rodings, The CB5: Camb 5D 15
Roedeer Cl. CB1: Che H 5F 23
Roland Cl. CB4: Camb 4D 13
Roman Court *CB4: Camb* *1D 13*
(off Hercules Cl.)
Roman Hill CB23: Bart 3B 26
Romsey M. CB1: Camb 4A 22
Romsey Rd. CB1: Camb 4B 22
Romsey Ter. CB1: Camb 4A 22
ROMSEY TOWN 4A 22
Ronald Rolph Ct. CB5: Camb 4C 14
Ropert Brooke Mus. & Orchard Tea Gdns. 4F 27
Rose Cres. CB2: Camb 2D 3 (2C 20)
Roseford Rd. CB4: Camb 3B 12
Roselea CB24: Imp 3B 6
Rosemary La. CB1: Camb 4E 23
ROSIE MATERNITY HOSPITAL 4F 29
Rosina Ct. CB1: Camb 4A 22
Ross St. CB1: Camb 4A 22
Rotherwick Way CB1: Camb 4B 30
Rothleigh Rd. CB1: Camb 2C 30
Round Chu. St. CB5: Camb 1D 3 (2C 20)
Rowans, The CB24: Milt 4B 8
Rowlinson Way CB5: Camb 1A 22
Roxburgh Rd. CB1: Camb 2D 13
Royal Albert Almshouses CB2: Camb 5E 21
Rush Gro. CB1: Che H 1F 31
Russell Cl. CB2: Camb 5D 21
Russell St. CB2: Camb 5E 21
Russet Cl. CB4: Ches 3B 14
Rustat Av. CB1: Camb 5F 21
Rustat Cl. CB1: Camb 5F 21
Rustat Rd. CB1: Camb 1F 29
Ruth Bagnall Ct. CB1: Camb 4A 22
Rutherford Rd. CB2: Camb 3D 29
Rutland Cl. CB4: Camb 3C 12

S

Sable Cl. CB1: Che H 5F 23
Sackville Cl. CB4: Camb 2D 13
Sadlers Cl. CB23: Cot 2A 18

Saffron Rd. CB24: His 3A 6
St Albans Rd. CB4: Camb 3C 12
St Andrew's Arc. CB2: Camb 3E 3 (3D 21)
St Andrews Glebe CB1: Che H 5E 23
St Andrew's Pk. CB24: His 1A 6
St Andrew's Rd. CB4: Ches 1F 21
St Andrew's St. CB2: Camb 3E 3 (3D 21)
St Andrews Way CB24: Imp 2D 7
St Anthonys Wlk. CB2: Camb 5D 21
St Audrey's Cl. CB24: His 2F 5
St Barnabas Ct. CB1: Camb 4F 21
St Barnabas Rd. CB1: Camb 4F 21
St Bartholomews Ct. CB5: Camb 1A 22
St Bede's Cres. CB1: Camb 1D 31
St Bede's Gdns. CB1: Camb 1D 31
St Catharines Hall CB23: Cot 2B 18
St Catharine's Rd. CB4: Camb 2C 12
St Catharine's Sq. CB4: Camb 2C 12
St Christopher's Av. CB3: Camb 5B 12
St Clements Gdns. CB5: Camb 1D 3
St David's Ho. CB4: Camb 5B 12
                                    (off Bermuda Rd.)
St Edward's Pas. CB2: Camb 3D 3 (3C 20)
St Eligius Pl. CB2: Camb 4D 21
St Eligius St. CB2: Camb 5D 21
St George's Ct. CB1: Camb 2F 29
St George's Way CB24: Imp 3D 7
St John's Innovation Cen. CB4: Camb 1B 14
St John's La. CB25: Horn 4F 9
St John's Pl. CB3: Camb 1B 20
St John's Rd. CB5: Camb 1D 3 (1C 20)
      CB23: Cot 2A 18
St John's St. CB2: Camb 2D 3 (2C 20)
St Kilda Av. CB4: Camb 2F 13
St Lukes M. CB4: Camb 1C 20
St Luke's St. CB4: Camb 1C 20
St Margaret's Rd. CB3: Girt 3E 11
St Margarets Sq. CB1: Camb 2A 30
St Marks Ct. CB3: Camb 4B 20
St Mary's Ct. CB2: Camb 2D 3
St Mary's Pas. CB2: Camb 3D 3 (3C 20)
St Mary's St. CB2: Camb 3D 3 (3C 20)
St Matthew's Ct. CB1: Camb 2F 21
St Matthew's Gdns. CB1: Camb 2F 21
St Matthew's St. CB1: Camb 2F 21
St Paul's Pl. CB1: Camb 4E 21
                                    (off St Paul's Wlk.)
St Paul's Rd. CB1: Camb 5F 3 (4E 21)
St Paul's Wlk. CB1: Camb 4E 21
St Peter's Rd. CB23: Cot 2A 18
St Peter's St. CB3: Camb 1B 2 (1B 20)
St Peter's Ter. CB2: Camb 5E 3 (4D 21)
St Philip's Rd. CB1: Camb 4A 22
St Regis CB4: Camb 5E 13
St Stephen's Pl. CB3: Camb 5B 12
St Thomas's Rd. CB1: Camb 1C 30
St Thomas's Sq. CB1: Camb 1C 30
St Vigor's Rd. CB21: Ful 3E 33
St Vincent's Cl. CB3: Girt 1D 11
Salisbury Pl. CB2: Trum 4C 28
Salisbury Vs. CB1: Camb 5E 21
Salmon La. CB1: Camb 2F 3 (2E 21)
Sanders La. CB21: Ful 3F 33
Sandwick Cl. CB4: Camb 1D 13
Sandy La. CB4: Camb 5E 13
Saxon Cl. CB24: Oak 1C 4
Saxon Rd. CB5: Camb 1F 21
Saxon St. CB2: Camb 5E 3 (4D 21)
Scarsdale Cl. CB4: Ches 3A 14
Scholars Wlk. CB4: Ches 5F 13
School Ct. CB1: Camb 4A 22
School Hill CB24: His 2A 6
School La. CB21: Ful 3E 33
      CB23: Bart 3A 26
      CB24: Imp 3B 6
Scotland Cl. CB4: Ches 4F 13
Scotland Rd. CB4: Ches 5F 13
Scotsdowne Rd. CB2: Trum 4C 28
Scott Polar Research Institute 5F 3 (4D 21)
Scroope Ter. CB2: Camb 5E 3 (4C 20)
Searle St. CB4: Camb 5C 12
Sedgewick Mus. of Earth Sciences 4E 3 (3D 21)
Sedgwick Cl. CB1: Camb 4A 22
Sedley Ct. CB1: Camb 5A 22
Sedley Taylor Rd. CB2: Camb 3E 29
Sefton Cl. CB2: Trum 4C 28
Selwyn Gdns. CB3: Camb 5A 2 (4A 20)

Selwyn Rd. CB3: Camb 5A 20
Senate Ho. Pas. CB2: Camb 3C 2 (3C 20)
Severn Pl. CB1: Camb 2F 21
Seymour Cl. CB1: Camb 4B 22
Seymour St. CB1: Camb 4B 22
Shaftesbury Rd. CB2: Camb 1E 29
SHELFORD BOTTOM 5C 30
Shelford Rd. CB2: Trum 5C 28
      CB21: Ful 5F 31
Shelly Gdn. CB3: Camb 1B 20
Shelly Row CB3: Camb 1B 20
Shenstone Ho. CB1: Camb 2F 21
                                    (off Staffordshire St.)
Shepherds Cl. CB1: Che H 1F 31
      CB5: Fen D 4E 15
Sheppard Flats CB3: Camb 1F 19
Sheppard Way CB1: Tev 3A 24
Sherbourne Cl. CB4: Ches 3A 14
Sherbourne Rd. CB4: Ches 3A 14
Sherlock Cl. CB3: Camb 5A 12
Sherlock Ct. CB3: Camb 5A 12
Sherlock Rd. CB3: Camb 4A 12
Sherman Ho. CB1: Camb 5F 21
Ship La. CB5: Camb 1D 3
                                    (off Thompson's La.)
Shirley Cl. CB24: Milt 4D 9
Shirley Gro. CB4: Ches 4A 14
Shirley Rd. CB24: His 3A 6
Short Drove Way CB21: Lit W 5F 17
Short St. CB1: Camb 2F 3 (2D 21)
Sidgwick Av. CB3: Camb 5A 2 (4B 20)
Sidney Farm Rd. CB1: Che H 1D 31
Sidney St. CB2: Camb 2D 3 (2C 20)
Signet Ct. CB5: Camb 1A 22
Silverdale Av. CB23: Cot 2A 18
Silverdale Cl. CB23: Cot 2A 18
Silver St. CB3: Camb 5C 2 (4C 20)
Silverwood Cl. CB1: Camb 2A 22
Simons Ho. CB4: Camb 5B 12
Sladwell Cl. CB3: Gran 4E 27
Sleaford St. CB1: Camb 3F 21
Somerset Cl. CB4: Camb 2C 12
Somerset Rd. CB24: His 3F 5
Somervell Ct. CB4: Camb 2D 13
Southacre Cl. CB2: Camb 1D 29
Southacre Dr. CB2: Camb 1D 29
Southbrooke Cl. CB2: Trum 4C 28
South Grn. Rd. CB3: Camb 5B 20
South Rd. CB24: Imp 5A 6
Southside CB4: Ches 4F 13
Sovereign Pl. CB4: Camb 2D 13
                                    (off Apollo Way)
Spalding Way CB1: Camb 3C 30
Speedwell Cl. CB1: Che H 1F 31
Spencer Ho. CB4: Camb 5B 12
                                    (off Bermuda Rd.)
Spens Av. CB3: Camb 4A 20
Spinney, The CB1: Camb 1B 30
Spring Cl. CB24: His 2B 6
Springfield Rd. CB4: Camb 5D 13
      CB24: Imp 5B 6
Springfield Ter. CB4: Camb 5D 13
Spurgeon's Cl. CB1: Tev 3A 24
Square, The CB25: Horn 5F 9
      CB25: Stow Q 3F 17
Stacey La. CB3: Camb 2F 19
Staffordshire Gdns. CB1: Camb 2F 21
                                    (off Staffordshire St.)
Staffordshire St. CB1: Camb 2F 21
Stanbury Cl. CB5: Fen D 3D 15
Stanesfield Cl. CB5: Camb 1C 22
Stanesfield Rd. CB5: Camb 1C 22
Stanley Av. CB4: Camb 1C 12
Stanley Ct. CB5: Camb 1A 22
Stanley Dr. CB4: Camb 1C 12
Stanley Rd. CB5: Camb 1A 22
Stansfield Gdns. CB21: Ful 2E 33
Stansgate Av. CB2: Camb 4A 30
Stanton Ho. CB1: Camb 2E 21
                                    (off Christchurch St.)
Stanway Cl. CB5: Camb 2E 21
Starling Cl. CB24: Milt 3C 8
Starr End CB4: Camb 1D 13
Station Rd. CB1: Camb 5E 21
      CB21: Ful 2F 33
      CB24: His 2A 6
      CB25: Stow Q 1D 17

Station Yd. CB21: Ful .1F **33**
Sterndale Cl. CB3: Girt 5D **5**
Sterne Cl. CB1: Camb .1A **30**
Stevenson Ct. CB5: Camb 1F **21**
Stevenson Ho. CB4: Camb 4F **13**
Stirling Cl. CB4: Ches 4F **13**
Stockwell St. CB1: Camb 4A **22**
Stonebridge La. CB21: Ful 3F **33**
Stone St. CB1: Camb .3A **22**
Stone Ter. CB1: Camb 3A **22**
Storey's Way CB3: Camb 5A **12**
Stott Gdns. CB4: Camb 3F **13**
Stourbridge Gro. CB1: Camb 3B **22**
Stow Cl. CB25: Stow Q 3E **17**
STOW CUM QUY 3F **17**
Stow Rd. CB25: Stow Q 4E **17**
Strangeways Rd. CB1: Camb 3C **30**
Stratfield Cl. CB4: Camb 4A **12**
Strathcarron Ct. CB4: Camb 2D **13**
Stretten Av. CB4: Camb 5C **12**
Stukeley Cl. CB3: Camb 4F **19**
Stulp Fld. Rd. CB3: Gran 3F **27**
Sturmer Cl. CB2: Camb 2C **12**
Sturton St. CB1: Camb 2F **21**
Suez Rd. CB1: Camb .5B **22**
(not continuous)
Summer Ct. CB5: Camb 1C **22**
Summerfield CB3: Camb 5B **2** (4B **20**)
Sunflower St. CB4: Camb 2C **12**
Sunmead Wlk. CB1: Che H 1F **31**
Sunningdale Cvn. Pk. CB4: Camb 3C **14**
Sunnyside CB5: Camb 2D **23**
Sunset Sq. CB4: Camb 2C **12**
Sun St. CB1: Camb 2F **21**
Sussex St. CB1: Camb 2E **3** (2D **21**)
Sutton Cl. CB24: Milt .3C **8**
Swann's Rd. CB5: Camb 5B **14**
Swann's Ter. CB1: Camb 4F **21**
Swifts Cnr. CB21: Ful .2E **33**
Sycamore Cl. CB1: Camb 1C **30**
Sycamores, The CB24: Milt 4B **8**
Sylvester Rd. CB3: Camb 3A **20**
Symonds Cl. CB24: His 2A **6**
Symonds La. CB3: Gran 3F **27**

T

Tabrum Cl. CB3: Gran 3E **27**
Talbot Ho. CB1: Che H 1E **31**
Tamarin Gdns. CB1: Che H 1F **31**
Taunton Cl. CB1: Camb 5C **22**
Tavistock Rd. CB4: Camb 3B **12**
Teasel Way CB1: Che H 2F **31**
Tedder Way CB4: Camb 3C **12**
Temple Ct. *CB1: Camb* 2F **21**
(off Severn Pl.)
CB4: Camb 2D **13**
(off Hercules Cl.)
Templemore Cl. CB1: Camb 3A **30**
Ten Acre Pl. CB5: Camb 5B **14**
Tenby Cl. CB1: Che H 1F **31**
Tenison Av. CB1: Camb 4E **21**
Tenison Ct. CB1: Camb 4F **21**
Tenison Rd. CB1: Camb 5F **21**
(not continuous)
Tennis Ct. Rd. CB2: Camb 4E **3** (3D **21**)
Tennis Ct. Ter. CB2: Camb 4E **3** (4C **20**)
Tenpin 1F **29**
Terrace, The *CB3: Camb* 1B **2**
(off St Peter's St.)
TEVERSHAM 3A **24**
Teversham Drift CB1: Che H 5F **23**
Teversham Rd. CB1: Ful, Tev 5C **24**
CB21: Ful 5C **24**
Teynham Cl. CB1: Camb 5C **22**
The . . . .
Names prefixed with 'The' for example 'The Avenue'
are indexed under the main name such as 'Avenue, The'
Thetford Ter. CB5: Camb 1D **23**
Thirleby Cl. CB4: Camb 4C **12**
Thistle St. CB4: Camb 2C **12**
Thoday St. CB1: Camb 4A **22**
Thomas Rd. CB21: Ful 2C **32**
Thompson's La. CB5: Camb 1D **3** (2C **20**)
(not continuous)
Thorleye Rd. CB5: Camb 2C **22**

Thornton Cl. CB3: Girt 3F **11**
Thornton Cl. CB3: Girt 3E **11**
Thornton Rd. CB3: Girt 2E **11**
Thornton Way CB3: Girt 3F **11**
Thorpe Way CB5: Camb 5D **15**
Thrift's Wlk. CB4: Ches 5A **14**
Thulborn Cl. CB1: Tev 3A **24**
Tillyard Way CB1: Camb 3C **30**
Tiptree Cl. CB5: Camb 5E **15**
Tiverton Way CB1: Camb 5B **22**
Tom Amey Ct. CB1: Camb 4A **22**
Tomkins Mead Nature Reserve 5C **8**
Topcliffe Way CB1: Camb 4B **30**
Topham Way CB4: Camb 3C **12**
Topper St. CB4: Camb 1D **13**
Tourist Info. Cen.
Cambridge .3D **3** (3C **20**)
Town Cl. CB21: Ful 2E **33**
Townsend Cl. CB24: Milt 3C **8**
Trafalgar Rd. CB4: Camb 1D **21**
Trafalgar St. CB4: Camb 1D **21**
Tram Yd., The *CB1: Camb* 3E **21**
(off Dover St.)
Tredegar Cl. CB4: Camb 3D **13**
Tredgold La. CB1: Camb 2E **21**
Trevone Pl. CB1: Camb 5C **22**
Tribune Ct. *CB4: Camb* 2D **13**
(off Apollo Way)
Trinity Hall Farm Ind. Est. CB4: Ches 2A **14**
Trinity La. CB2: Camb 3C **2** (3C **20**)
Trinity St. CB2: Camb 3D **3** (2C **20**)
Tripos Ct. CB2: Camb 1E **29**
TRUMPINGTON 4C **28**
Trumpington (Park & Ride) 5B **28**
Trumpington Rd. CB2: Camb 5E **3** (3C **28**)
Trumpington St. CB2: Camb 4D **3** (3C **20**)
Trust Ct. CB24: His 4A **6**
Turpyn Ct. CB4: Camb 2D **13**
Tuscan Ct. CB4: Ches 4F **13**
Tweedale CB1: Che H .2E **31**
Tweedsmuir Ct. *CB4: Camb* 2D **13**
(off Banff Cl.)
Twickenham Ct. *CB4: Camb* 4E **13**
(off Arbury Rd.)

U

Union La. CB4: Ches 4E **13**
Union Rd. CB2: Camb 5F **3** (4D **21**)
University Botanic Garden 5D **21**
University Cricket Ground (Fenners) 4E **21**
University Library 3A **2** (3B **20**)
University of Cambridge 1F **19**
Unwin Sq. CB4: Camb 1C **12**
Uphall Rd. CB1: Camb 3C **22**
Up. Gwydir St. CB1: Camb 3F **21**

V

Valerian Ct. CB1: Che H 2F **31**
Velos Wlk. *CB5: Camb* 5D **15**
(off Ann's Rd.)
Ventress Cl. CB1: Camb 2C **30**
Ventress Farm Ct. CB1: Camb 2D **31**
Verulam Way CB4: Camb 2C **12**
Vicarage Dr. CB3: Gran 3F **27**
Vicarage Ter. CB1: Camb 3F **21**
Victoria Av. CB4: Camb 5D **13**
CB5: Camb 1F **3** (1D **21**)
Victoria Homes CB4: Camb 5D **13**
Victoria Pk. CB4: Camb 5C **12**
Victoria Rd. CB4: Camb 1B **20**
Victoria St. CB1: Camb 3F **3** (3D **21**)
Villa Ct. CB4: Camb 1D **13**
Villa Pl. CB24: Imp 4B **6**
Villa Rd. CB24: Imp 4B **6**
Vinery Pk. CB1: Camb 3B **22**
(Danesbury Ct.)
CB1: Camb 4B **22**
(Vinery Rd.)
Vinery Rd. CB1: Camb 4B **22**
Vinery Way CB1: Camb 3B **22**
Vines, The CB24: Oak .1B **4**
Vinter Ter. CB2: Camb 5E **21**
Violet Cl. CB1: Che H .2F **31**

Vision Pk. CB24: His 4A 6
Vue Cinema
  Cambridge 2E 21

W

Wadloes Footpath CB5: Fen D 5D 15
Wadloes Rd. CB5: Camb 5C 14
Wagstaff Cl. CB4: Camb 2E 13
Walker Ct. CB4: Camb 3D 13
Walkling Way CB24: Milt 4C 8
Walnut Cl. CB24: Milt 4B 8
Walnut Tree Av. CB5: Camb 1F 21
Walnut Tree Way CB4: Camb 2B 12
Walpole Rd. CB1: Camb 2C 30
Ward Rd. CB1: Camb 1C 30
Warkworth St. CB1: Camb 3F 3 (3E 21)
Warkworth Ter. CB1: Camb 3F 3 (3E 21)
Warren Cl. CB1: Camb 5E 21
Warren Rd. CB4: Camb 4F 13
Warwick Rd. CB4: Camb 4B 12
Washpit Rd. CB3: Girt 1B 10
Waterhouse CB4: Ches 5A 14
Water La. CB4: Ches 4A 14
  CB24: Imp 3B 6
  CB24: Oak 1B 4
Water St. CB4: Ches 5A 14
                                (not continuous)
Water Vw. CB5: Camb 1A 22
Wavell Way CB4: Camb 3D 13
Weavers Fld. CB3: Girt 2D 11
Wedgewood Dr. CB1: Che H 1E 31
Wellbrook Ct. CB3: Girt 2E 11
Wellbrook Way CB3: Girt 2E 11
Wellington Cl. CB1: Camb 2F 21
Wellington Pas. CB1: Camb 2F 21
                             (off Wellington Ct.)
Wellington St. CB1: Camb 2E 21
Welstead Rd. CB1: Che H 1F 31
Wentworth Rd. CB4: Camb 5A 12
Wenvoe Cl. CB1: Che H 1E 31
Westberry Ct. CB3: Camb 4A 20
Westbrook Cen. CB4: Camb 5D 13
Westering, The CB5: Camb 1D 23
Westfield La. CB4: Camb 5B 12
Westfield Rd. CB4: Camb 5B 12
West Gdns. CB3: Camb 4A 2 (3B 20)
Westgate CB1: Camb 2D 31
                                (off Carrick Cl.)
Weston Gro. CB21: Ful 2D 33
West Rd. CB3: Camb 4A 2 (3B 20)
  CB24: His 3A 6
Wests Renault Pk. 5F 19
West Vw. CB3: Camb 5B 20
Wetenhall Rd. CB1: Camb 4A 22
Wheaton Ho. CB1: Camb 2F 21
                            (off Staffordshire St.)
Wheeler St. CB2: Camb 3D 3 (3C 20)
Wheelwright Way CB25: Stow Q 3F 17
Whipple Mus. of The History of Science ...4D 3 (3C 20)
Whitefriars CB4: Ches 4A 14
Whitegate Cl. CB3: Girt 1D 11
Whitehill Cl. CB5: Camb 2C 22
Whitehill Rd. CB5: Camb 1B 22
Whitehouse La. CB3: Camb 4F 11
White Rose Wlk. CB4: Camb 2C 12
Whitfield Cl. CB4: Camb 2E 13
Whitgift Rd. CB1: Tev 4A 24
Whitwell Way CB23: Cot 2A 18

Whytford Cl. CB4: Ches 1F 21
Widnall Cl. CB3: Gran 3E 27
Wilberforce Rd. CB3: Camb 2A 20
Wilbraham Rd. CB21: Ful 1F 33
Wilderspin Cl. CB3: Girt 3E 11
Wilding Wlk. CB4: Ches 4F 13
Wiles Cl. CB4: Camb 2F 13
Wilkinson Pl. CB2: Camb 1E 29
Wilkin St. CB1: Camb 4F 21
William Smith Cl. CB1: Camb 5F 21
Willis Rd. CB1: Camb 3E 21
Willowbank CB4: Ches 1F 21
Willow Cres. CB24: Milt 4C 8
Willow Wlk. CB1: Camb 2F 3 (2E 21)
Wilson Cl. CB4: Camb 3F 13
Wilson Way CB24: Milt 4C 8
Wimpole Rd. CB23: Bart 4A 26
Winchmore Dr. CB2: Trum 4B 28
Windermere Cl. CB1: Che H 5F 23
Winders La. CB24: His 1A 6
Windlesham Cl. CB4: Camb 3D 13
Windmill La. CB21: Ful 2D 33
  CB24: His 2A 6
Windrush Cvn. Pk. CB1: Che H 1A 32
Windsor Rd. CB4: Camb 4A 12
Wingate Cl. CB1: Camb 4C 28
Wingate Way CB2: Trum 4C 28
Winship Rd. CB24: Milt 5B 8
Winstanley Ct. CB1: Camb 3A 22
Woburn Cl. CB4: Camb 2D 13
Wolfson Flats CB3: Camb 5A 12
Wollaston Rd. CB1: Camb 3E 21
Wolsey Way CB1: Che H 5E 23
Woodcock Cl. CB24: Imp 3C 6
Woodend CB2: Trum 5A 28
Woodhead Dr. CB4: Camb 3E 13
Woodhouse Way CB4: Camb 2F 13
Woodlands Cl. CB3: Girt 5C 4
Woodlands Pk. CB3: Girt 5C 4
Woodlark Rd. CB3: Camb 4A 12
Woodman Way CB24: Milt 4C 8
Woodvale Lodge CB4: Camb 1E 21
                             (off Manhattan Dr.)
Woody Grn. CB3: Girt 1D 11
Wootton Way CB3: Camb 4F 19
Wordsworth Gro. CB3: Camb 5B 2 (4B 20)
Worts C'way. CB1: Camb 4B 30
Wright's Cl. CB5: Fen D 3D 15
Wrights Gro. CB21: Ful 3E 33
WT Snooker & Sporting Club 2E 21
Wulfstan Ct. CB1: Camb 3B 30
Wulfstan Way CB1: Camb 3B 30
Wycliffe Rd. CB1: Camb 4B 22
Wyman's La. CB3: Camb 1B 20
Wynborne Cl. CB4: Camb 4D 13
Wynford Way CB4: Camb 2D 13

Y

Yarrow Rd. CB1: Che H 2F 31
York St. CB1: Camb 2F 21
York Ter. CB1: Camb 3F 21
Youngman Av. CB24: His 1B 6
Youngman Cl. CB24: His 1B 6
Young St. CB1: Camb 2F 21

Z

Zetland Wlk. CB1: Camb 5C 22

CAMBRIDGE UNIVERSITY COLLEGES & HALLS

covered by this atlas

with their map square reference

Christ's College 2E **3** (2D **21**)
Churchill College 1A **20**
Clare College 3C **2** (3C **20**)
Clare Hall 3A **2** (3A **20**)
Corpus Christi College 4D **3** (3C **20**)

Darwin College 5C **2** (4C **20**)
Downing College 5E **3** (4D **21**)

Emmanuel College 3F **3** (3D **21**)

Fitzwilliam College .5A **12**

Girton College 3E **11**
Gonville & Caius College 2C **2** (2C **20**)

Homerton College 2F **29**
Hughes Hall 4E **21**

Jesus College 1F **3** (2D **21**)

King's College 3C **2** (3C **20**)

Lucy Cavendish College 1A **2** (1B **20**)

Magdalene College 1C **2** (1C **20**)
Murray Edwards College .1B **20**

Newnham College 5A **2** (4B **20**)

Pembroke College 4D **3** (3C **20**)
Peterhouse 5D **3** (4C **20**)

Queen's College 4C **2** (3C **20**)

Robinson College 3A **2** (3A **20**)

St Catharine's College 4D **3** (3C **20**)
St Edmund's College 1B **20**
St John's College 1C **2** (2C **20**)
Selwyn College 5A **2** (4B **20**)
Sidney Sussex College 2D **3** (2D **21**)

Trinity College 2C **2** (2C **20**)
Trinity Hall 2C **2** (3C **20**)

Wolfson College 4A **20**